For permissions contact: support@oshidori.co

ISBN: 978-1-7350977-5-6 (paperback)
ISBN: 978-1-7350977-8-7 (ebook)

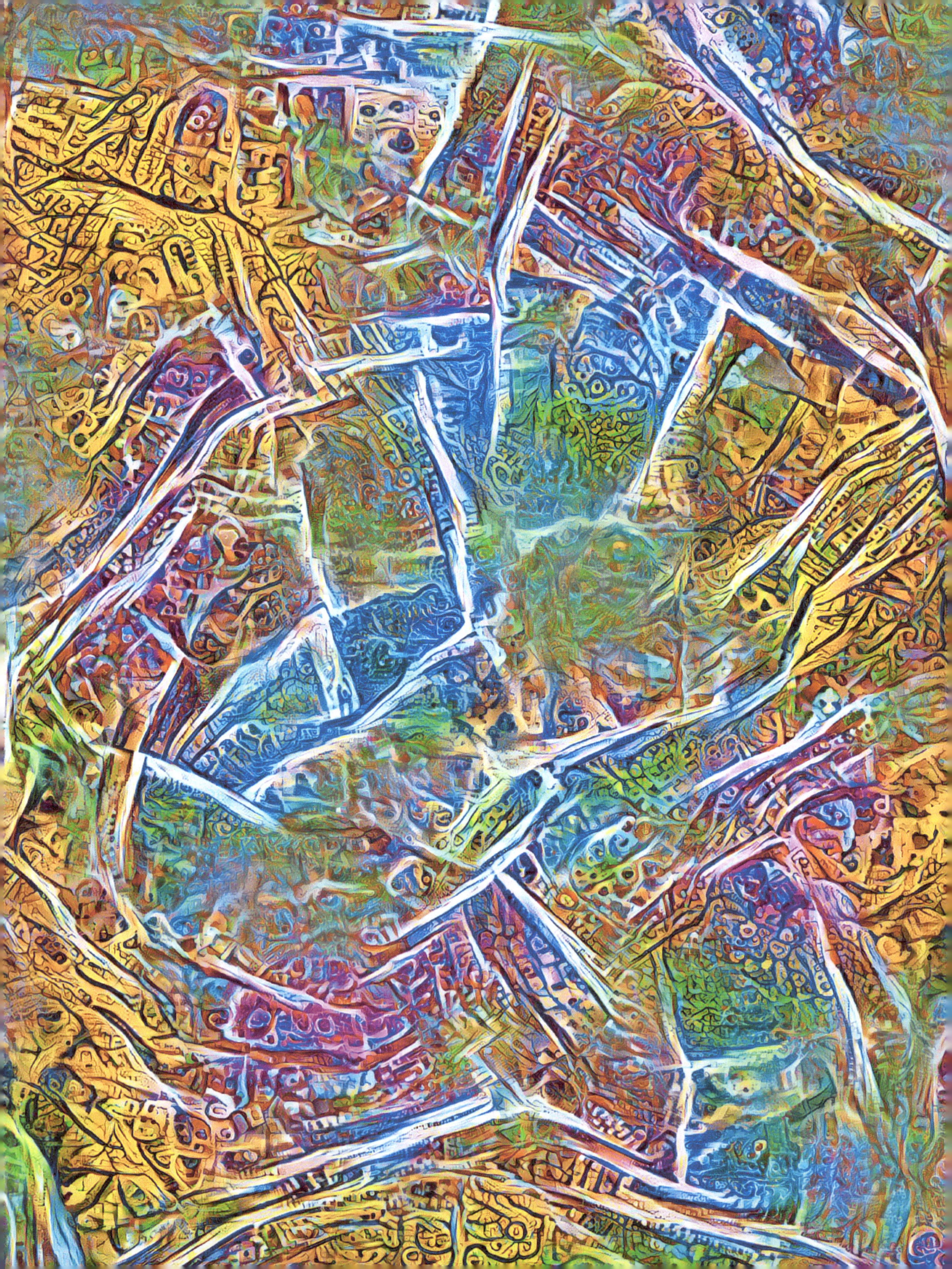

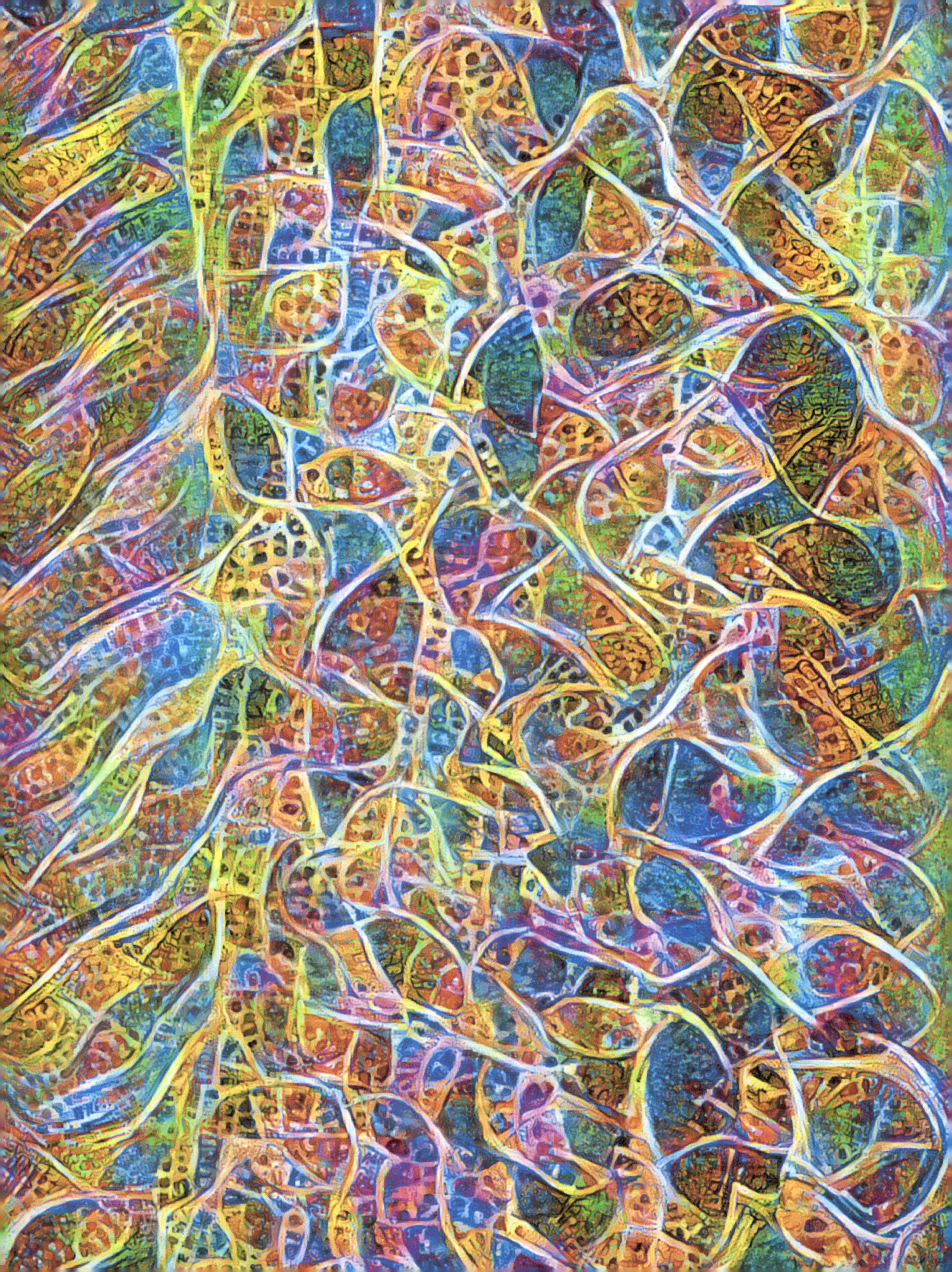

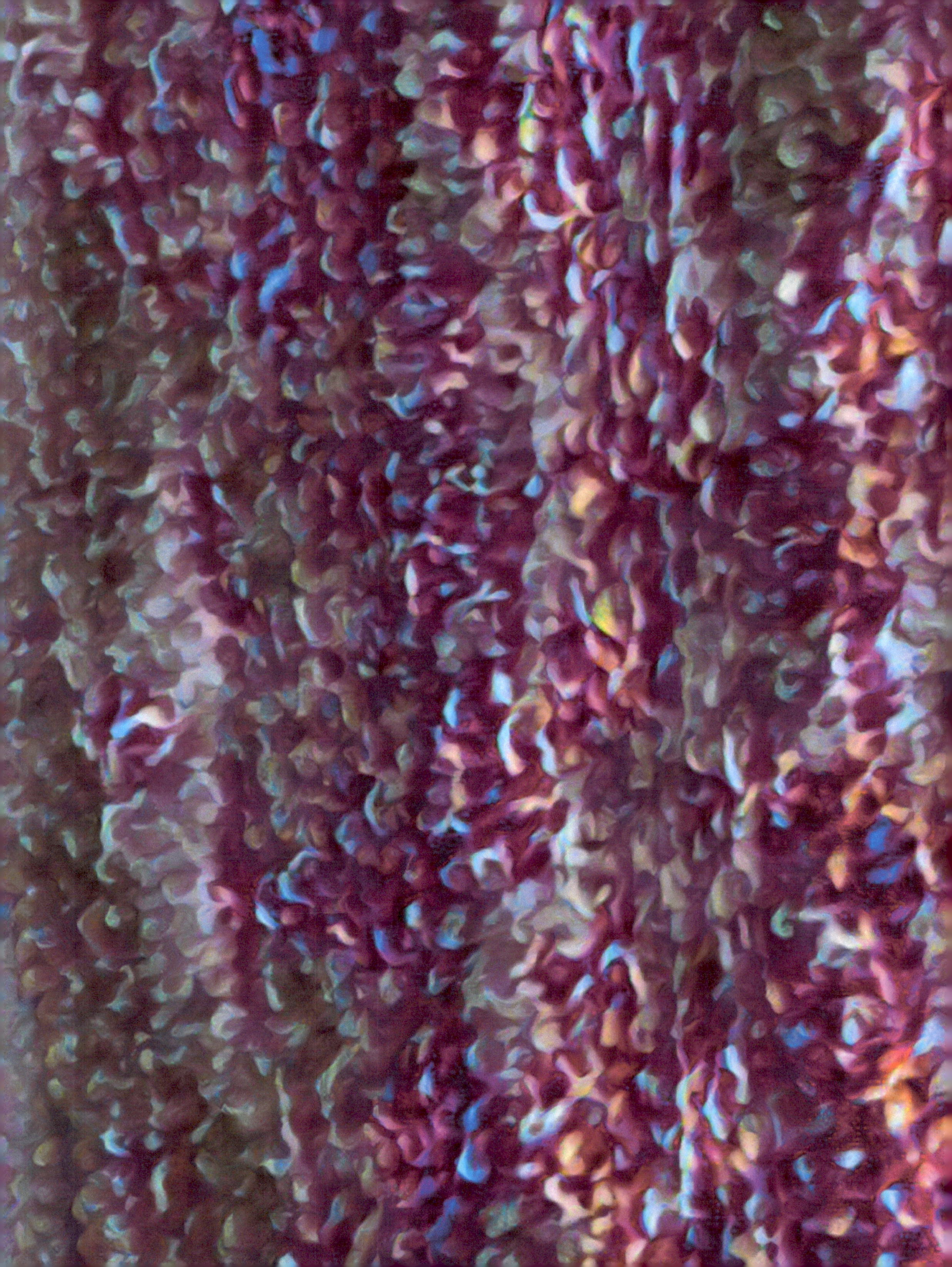

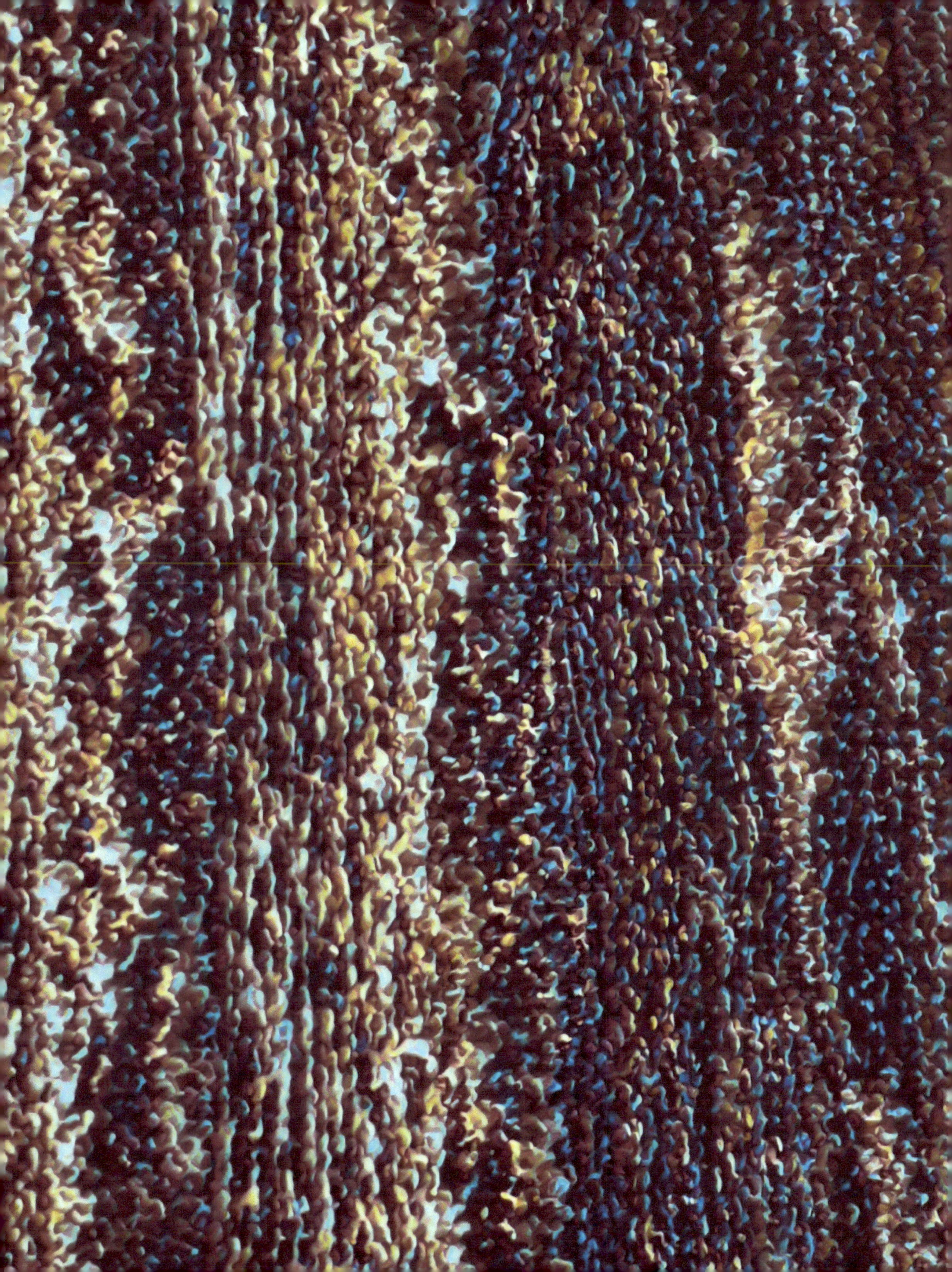

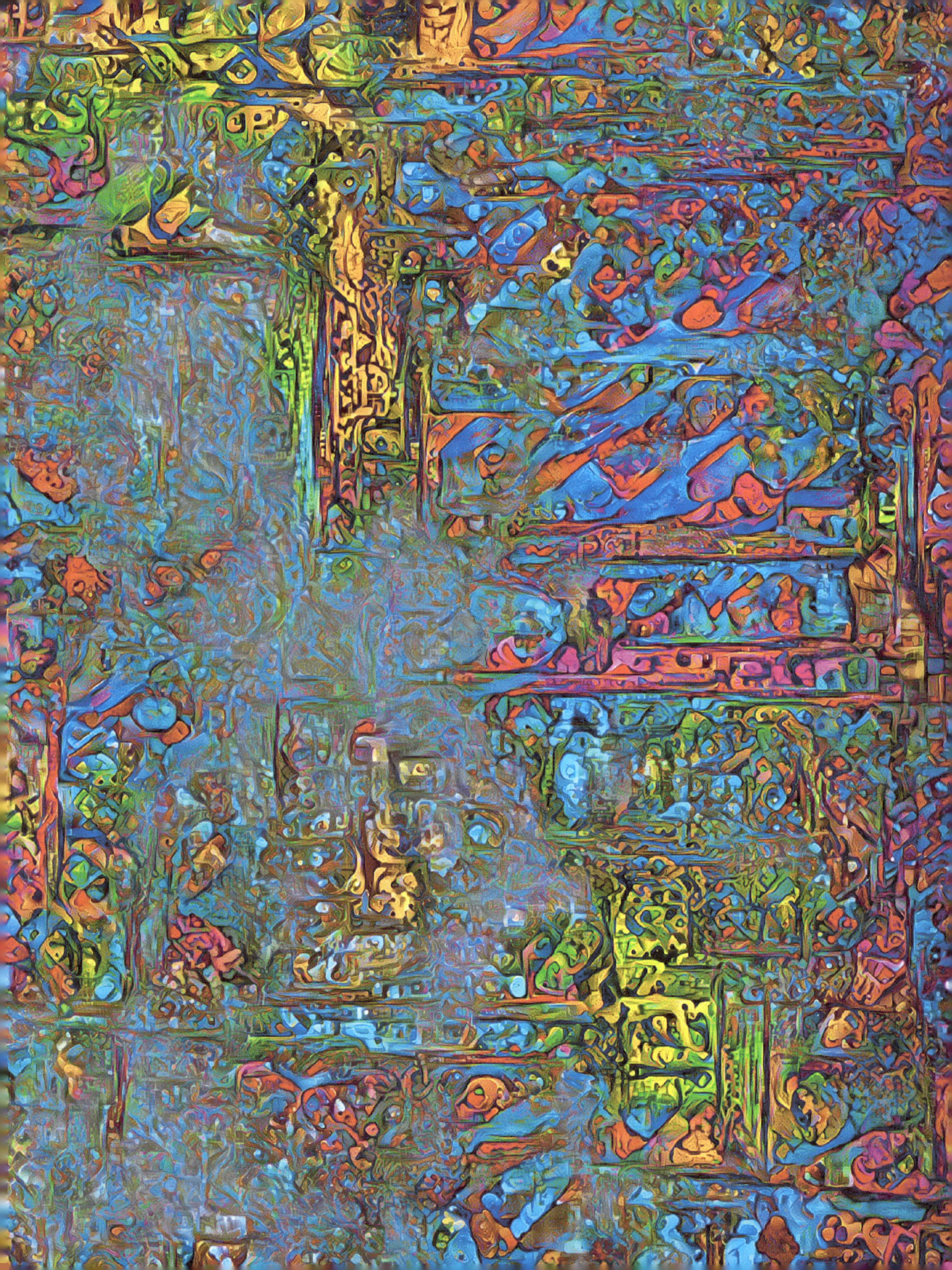

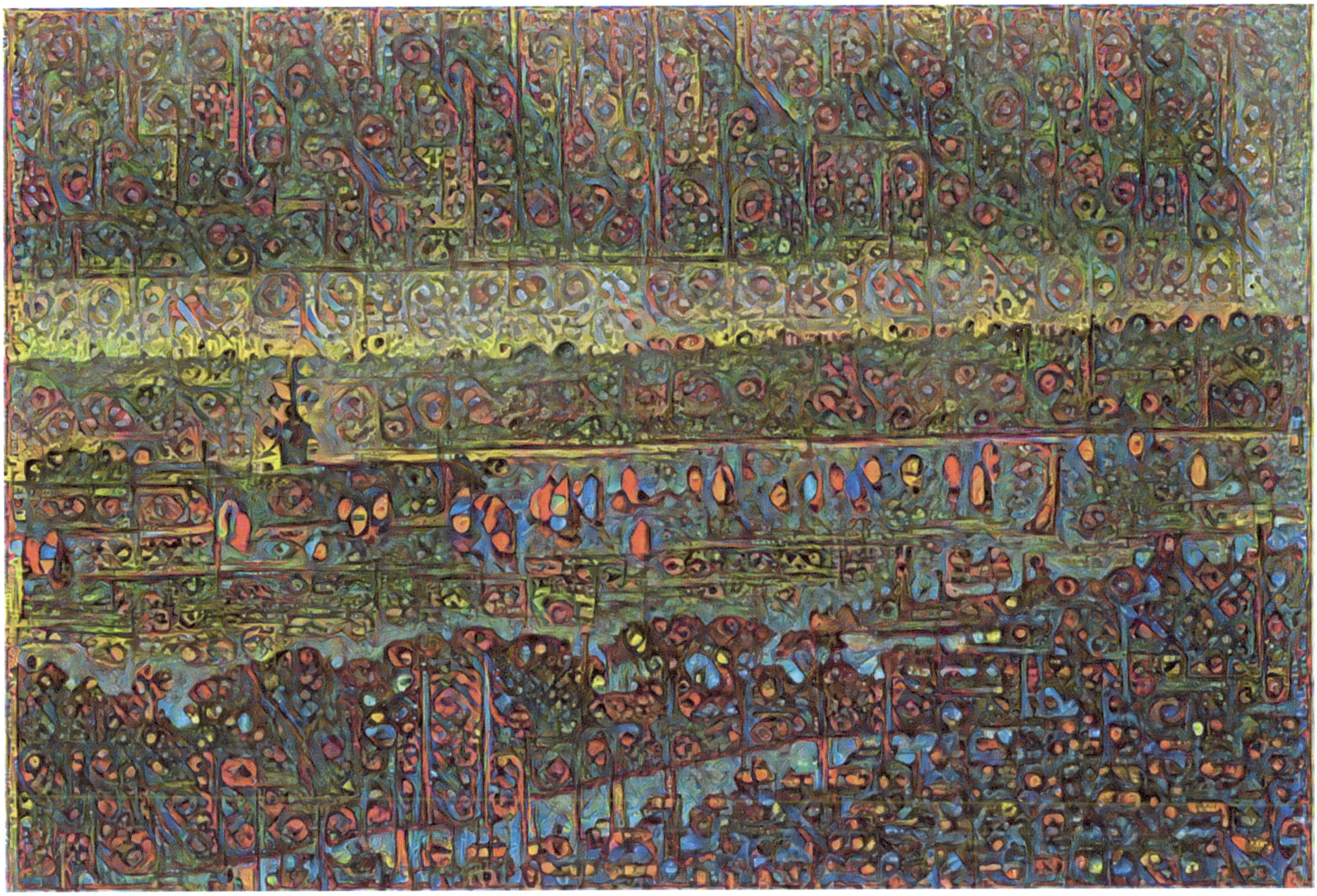

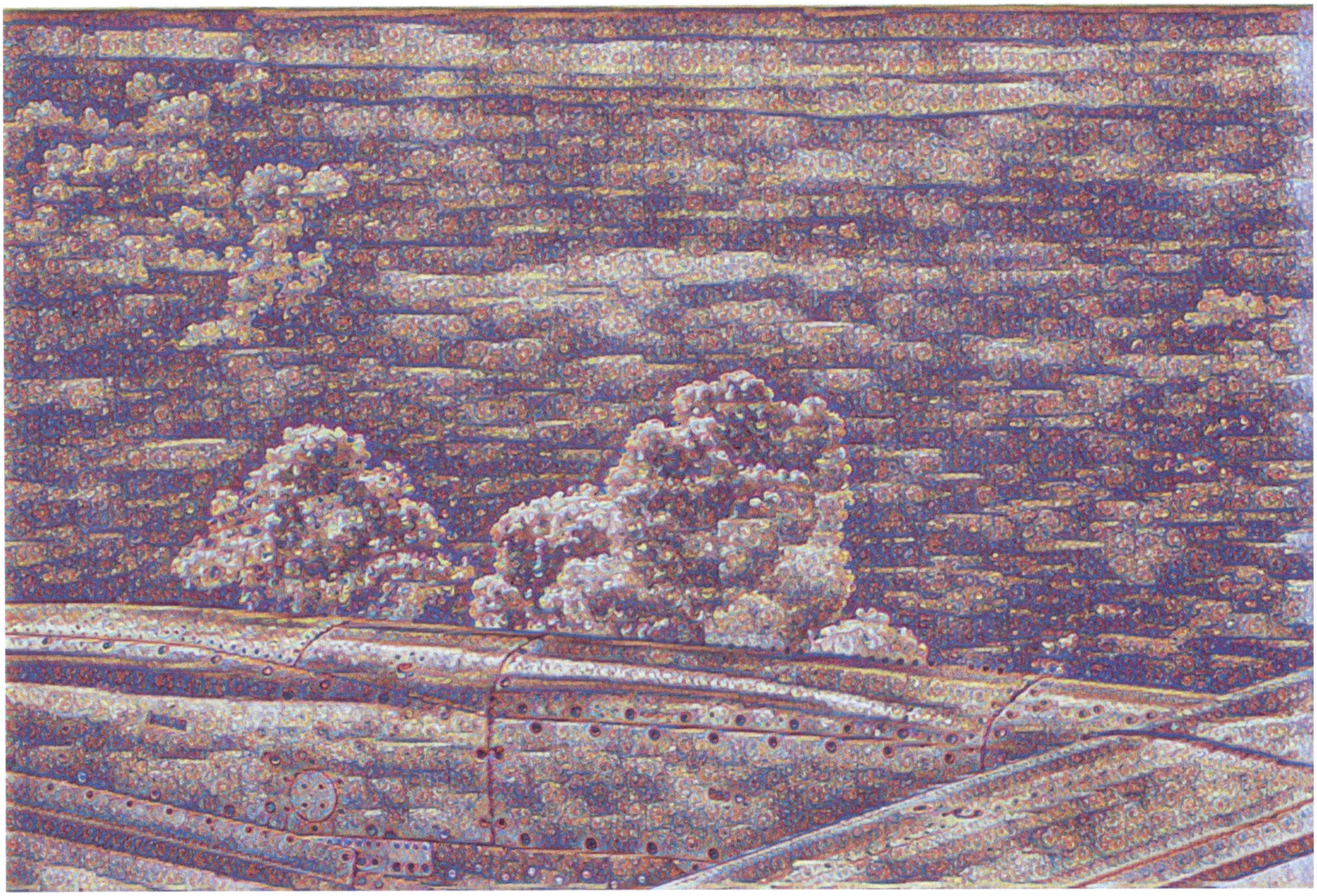

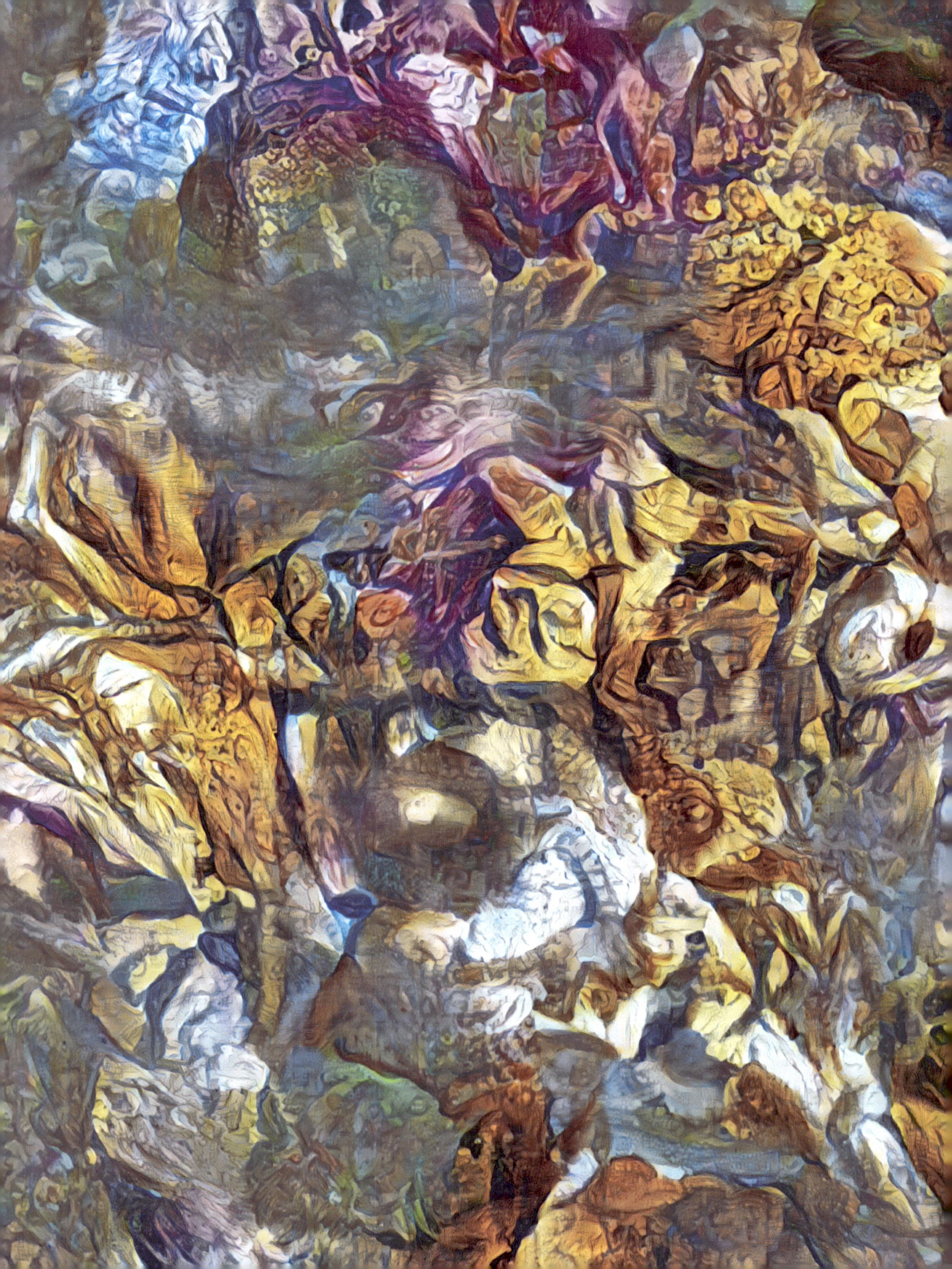

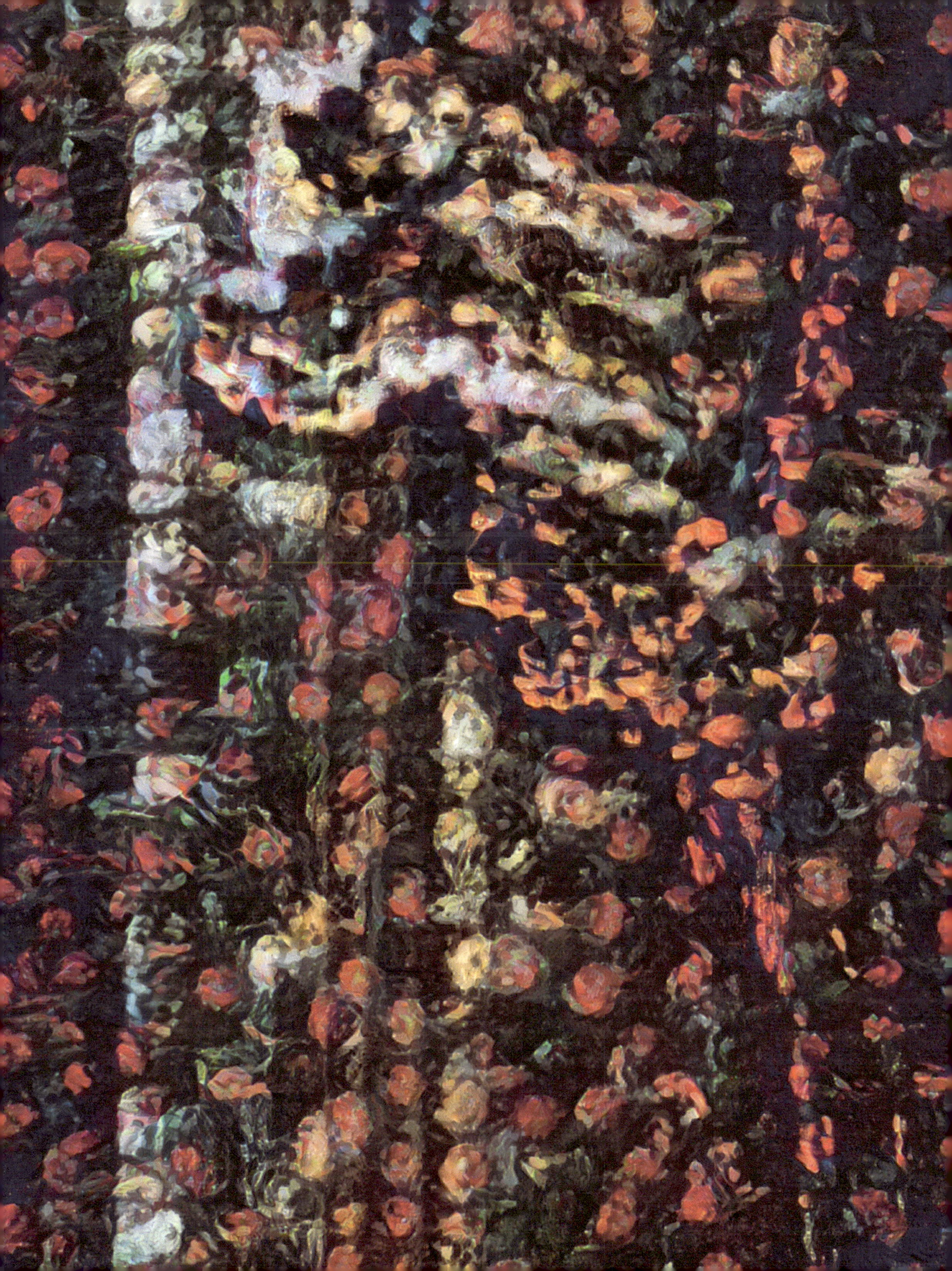

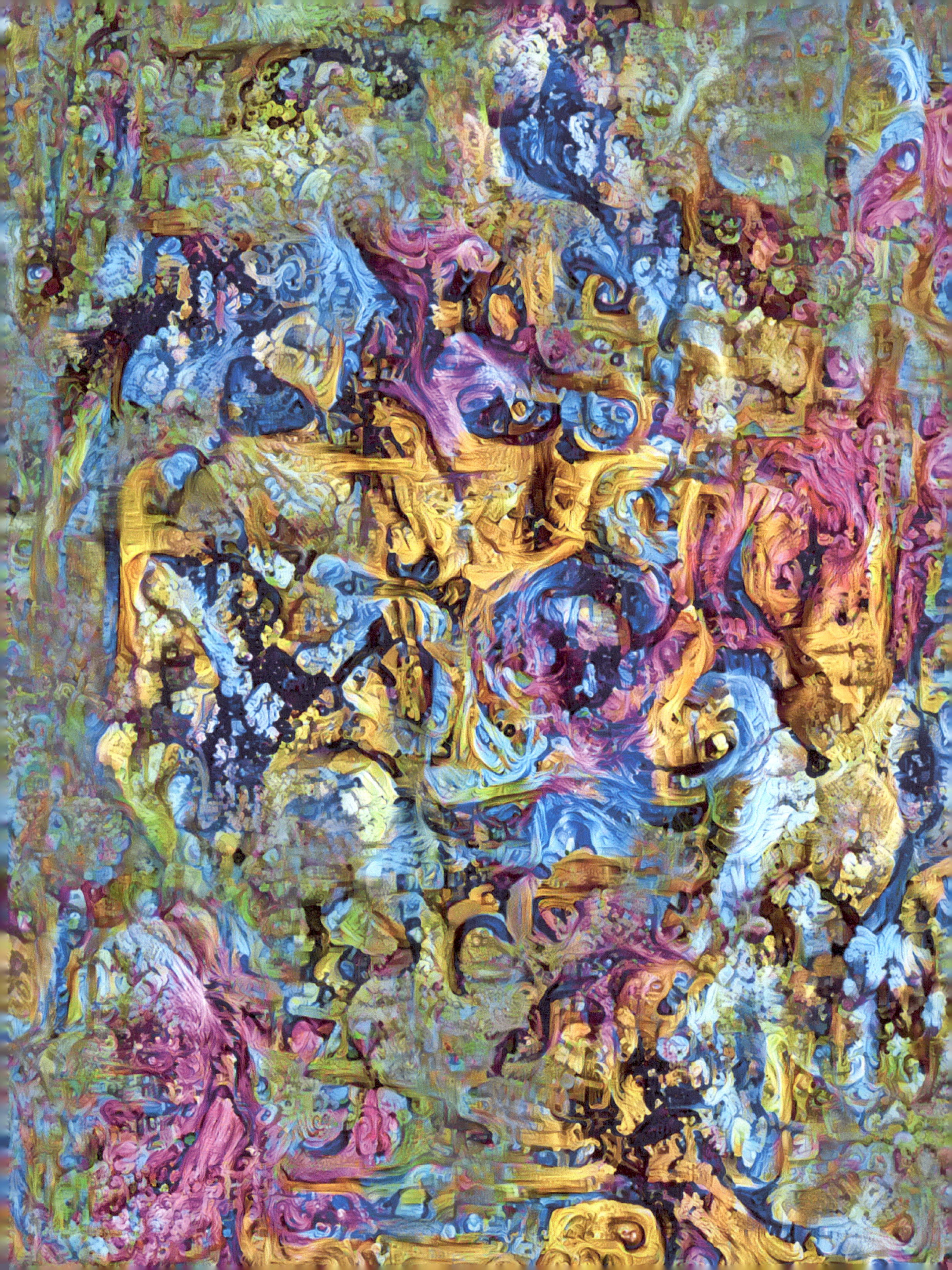

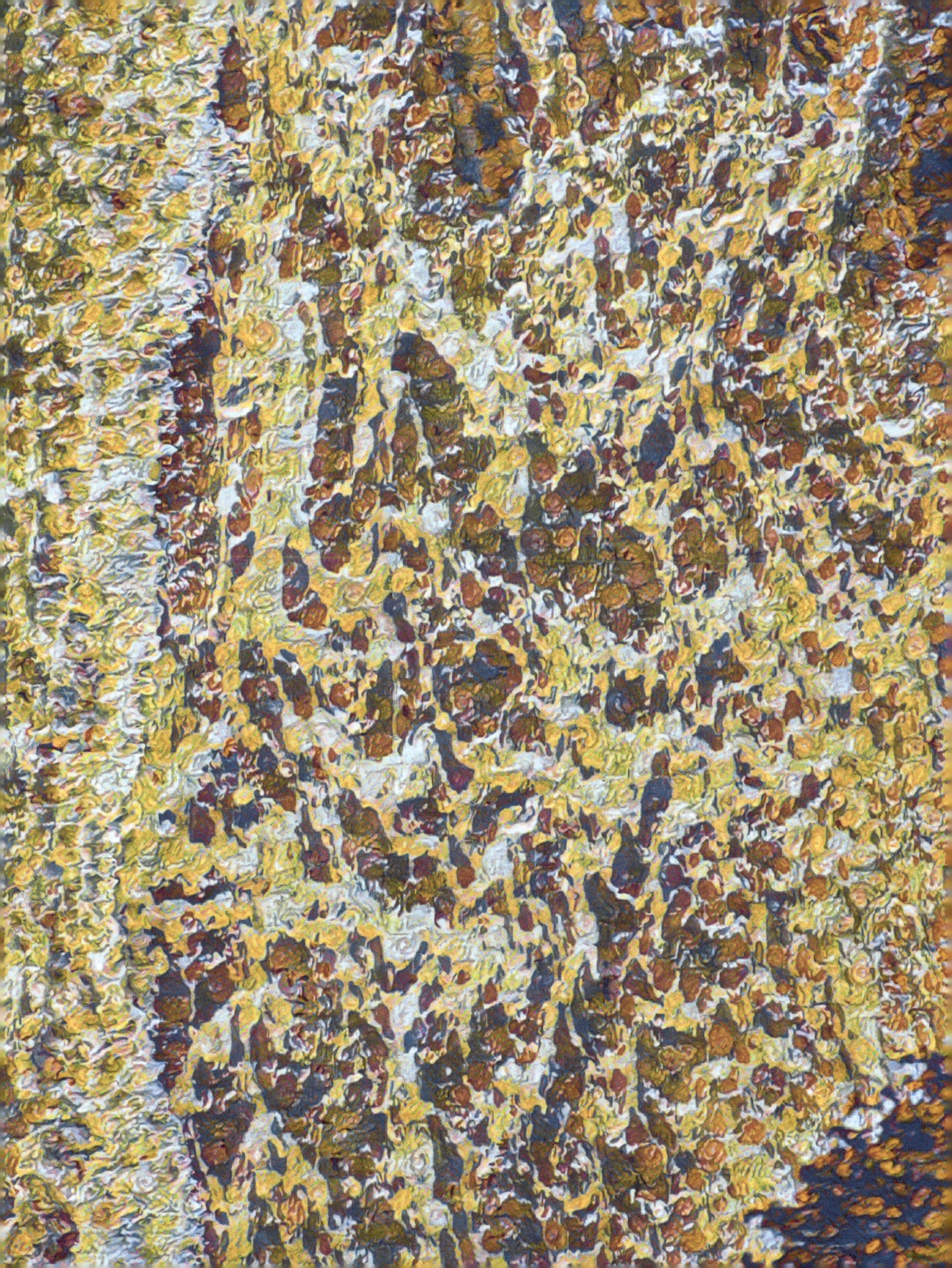

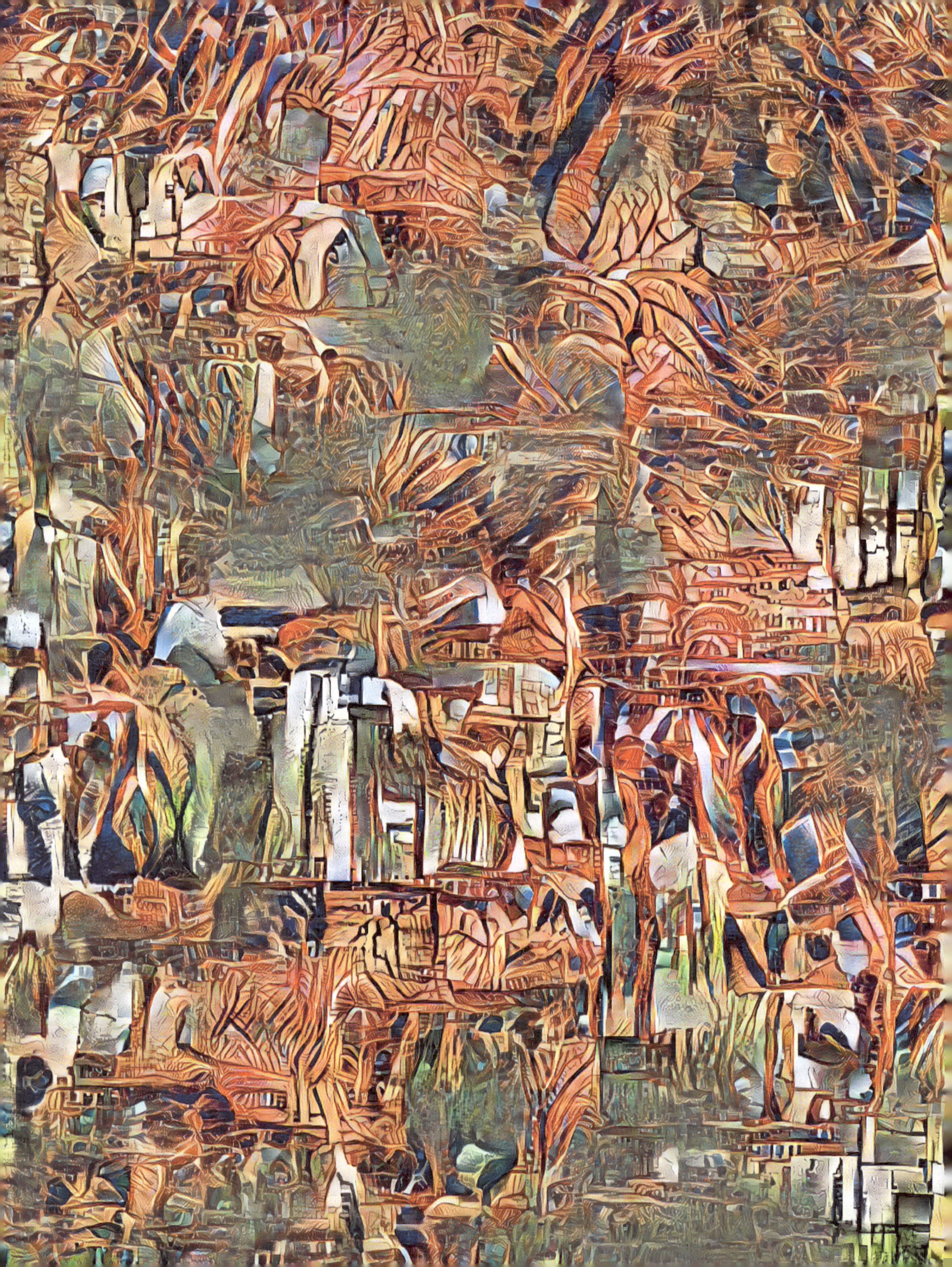

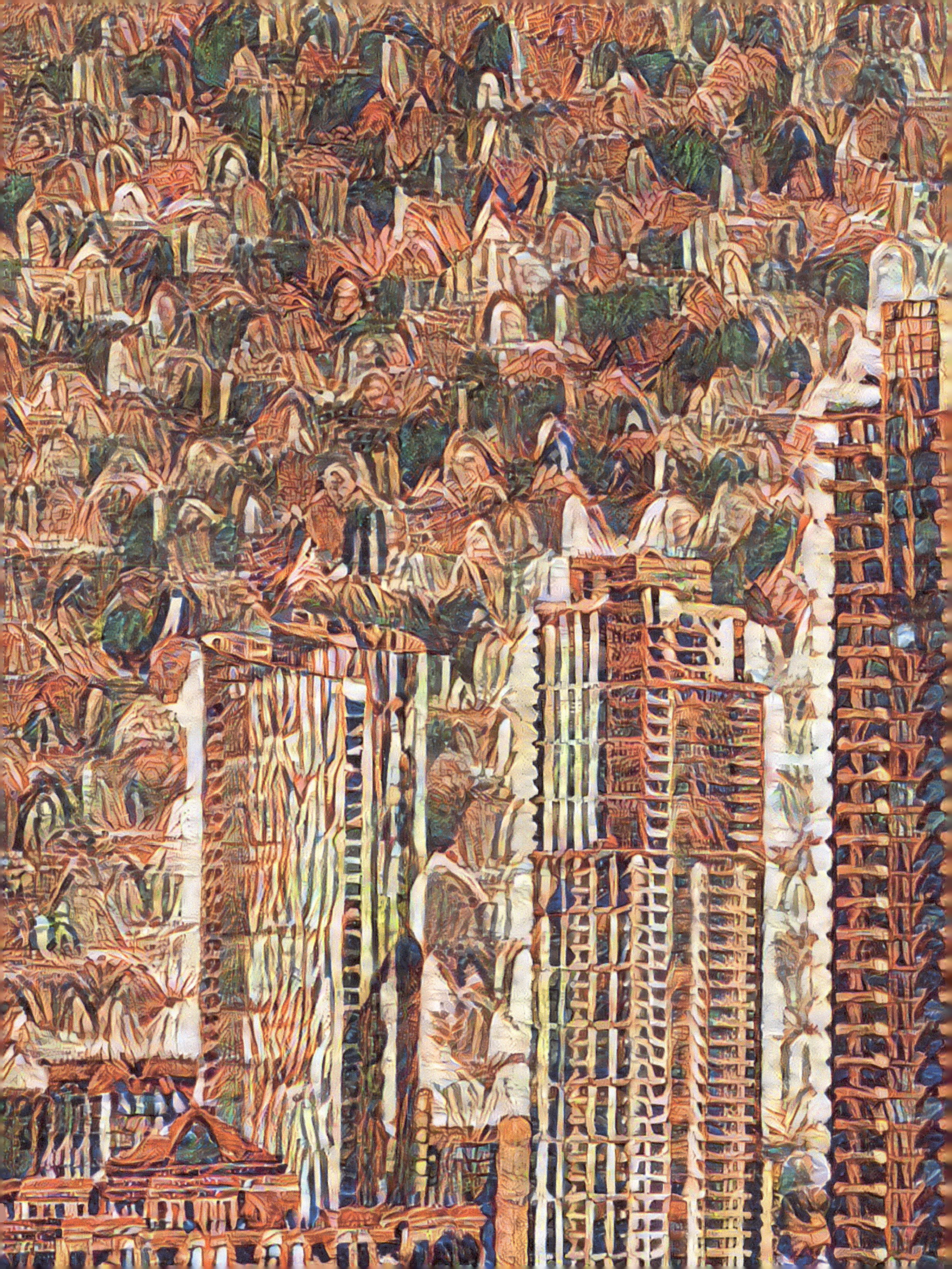

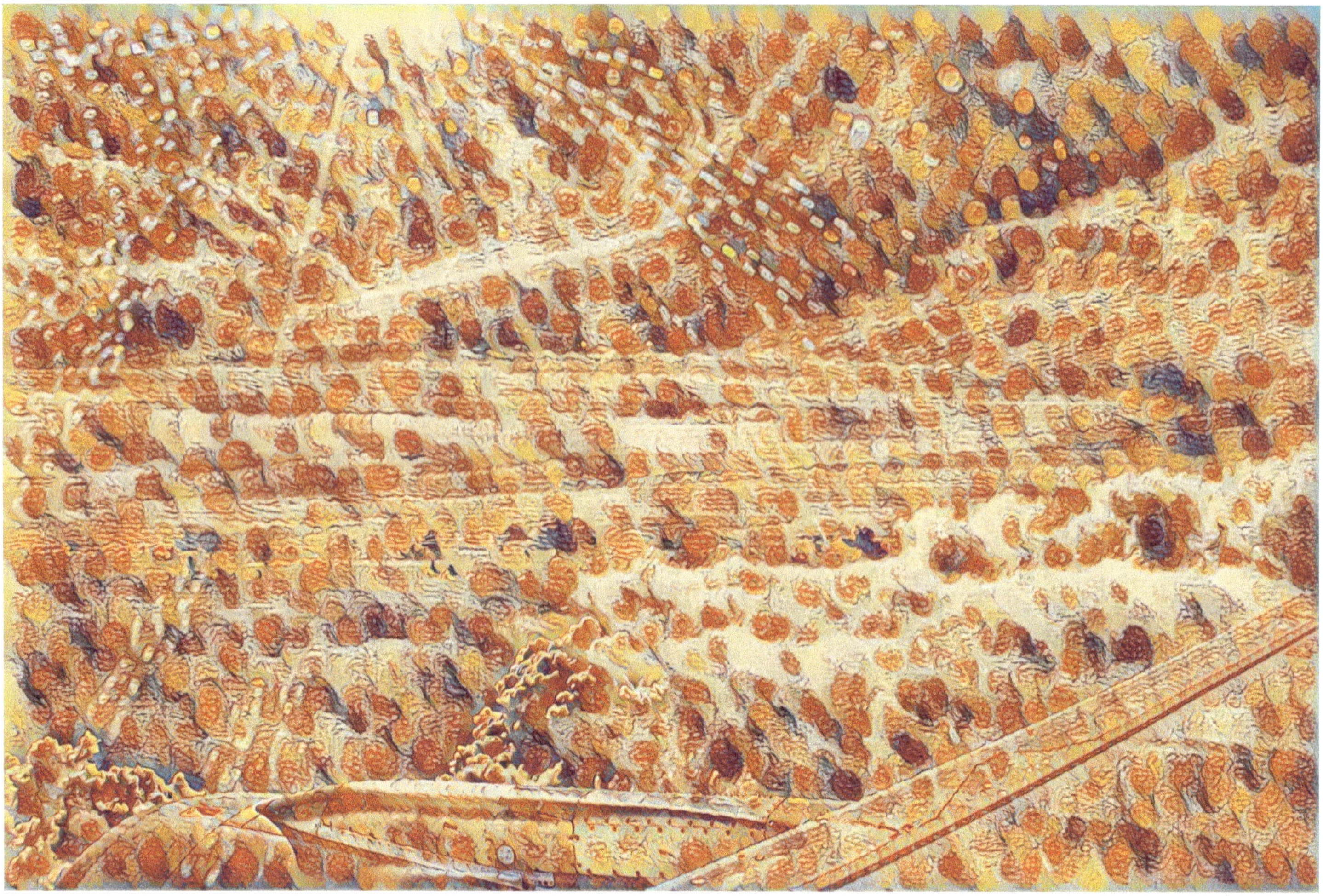

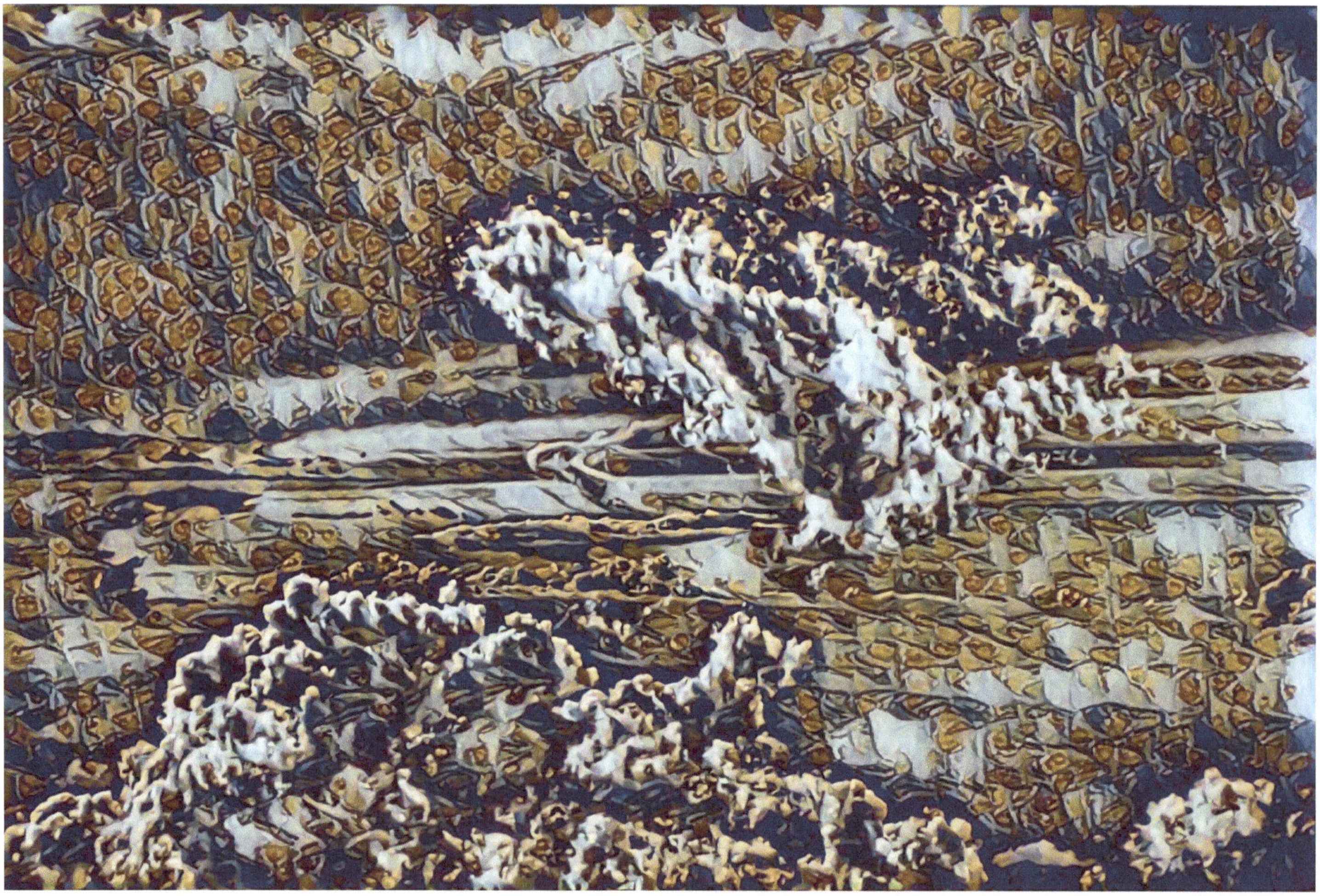

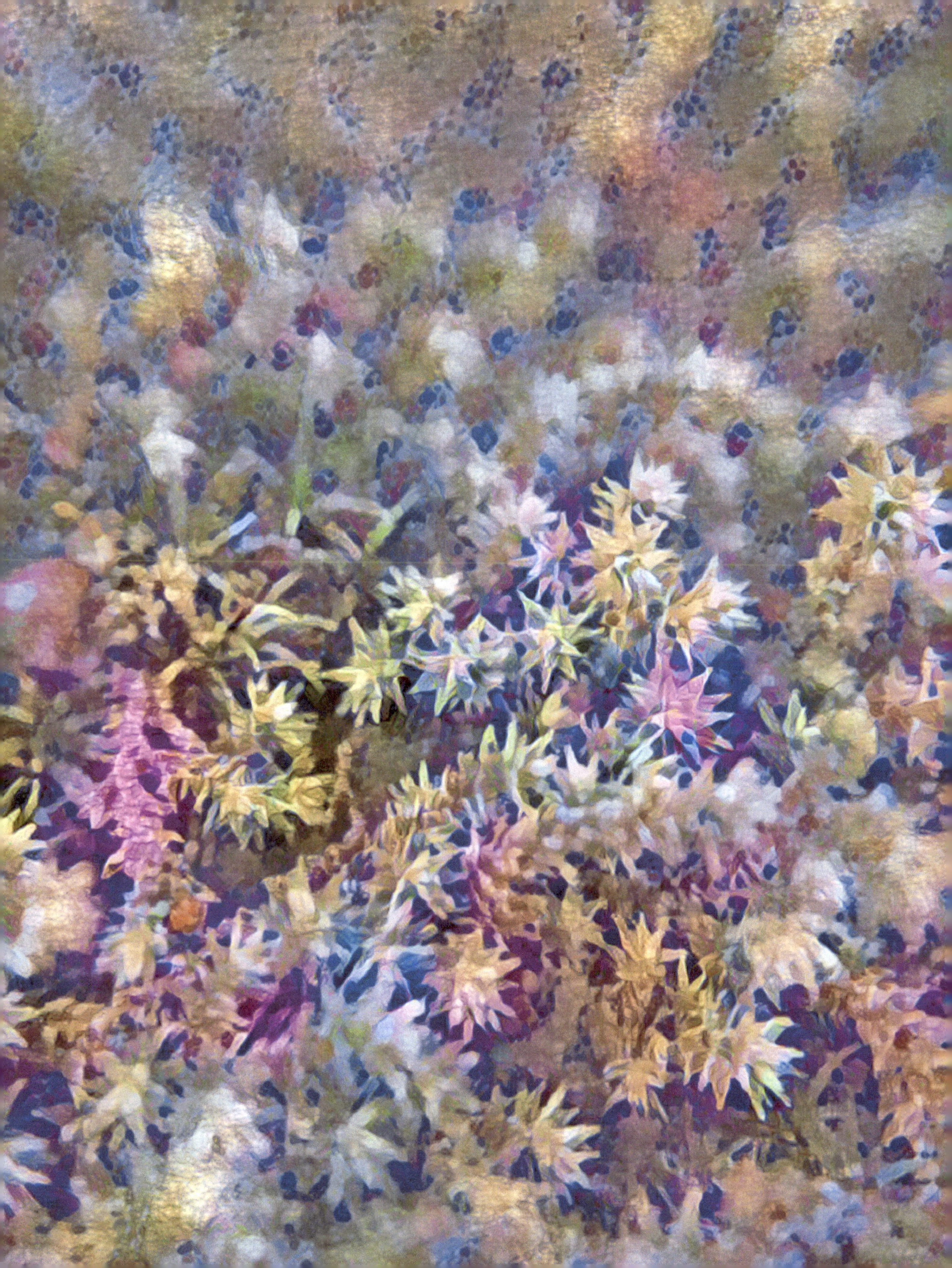

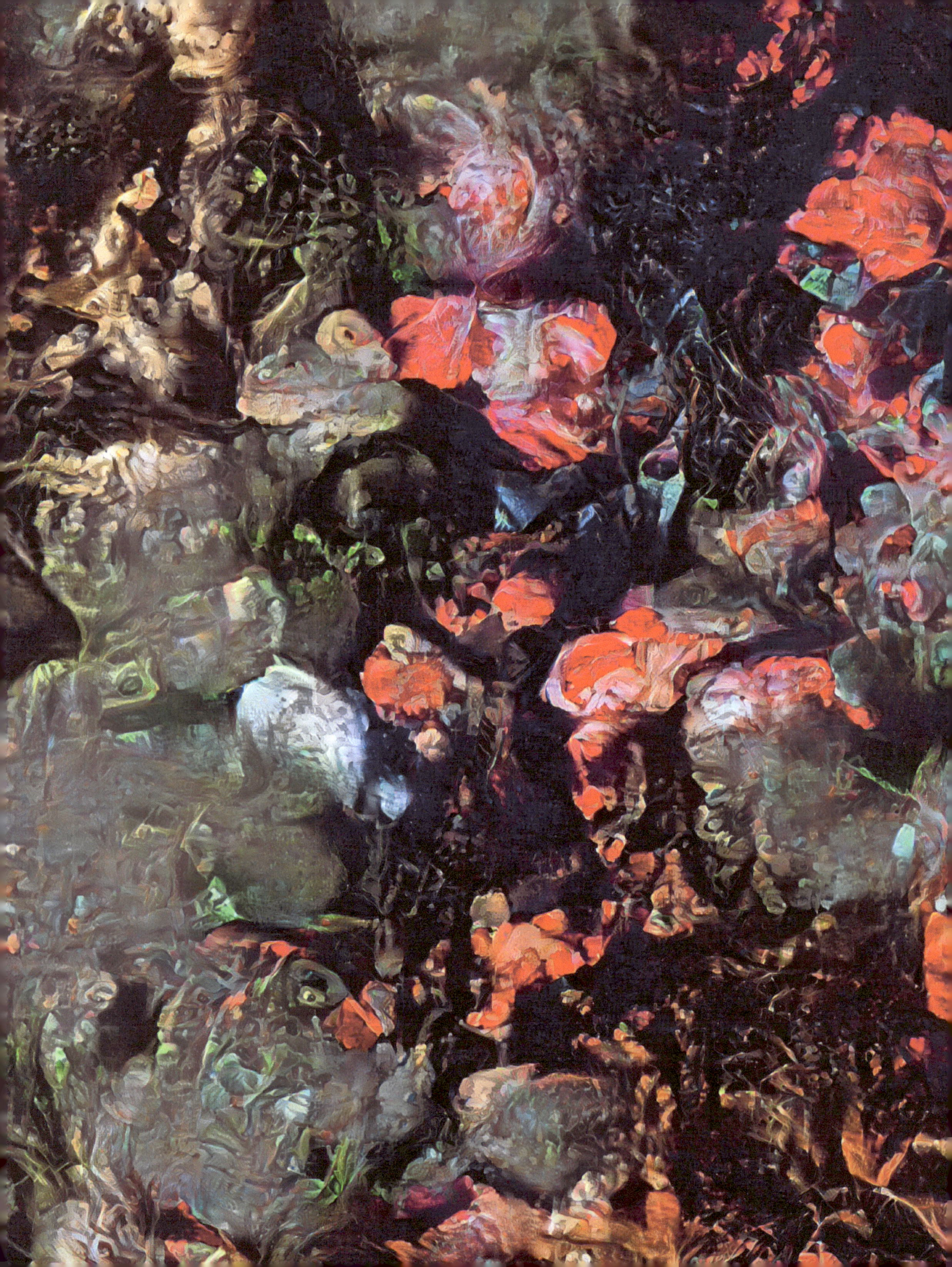

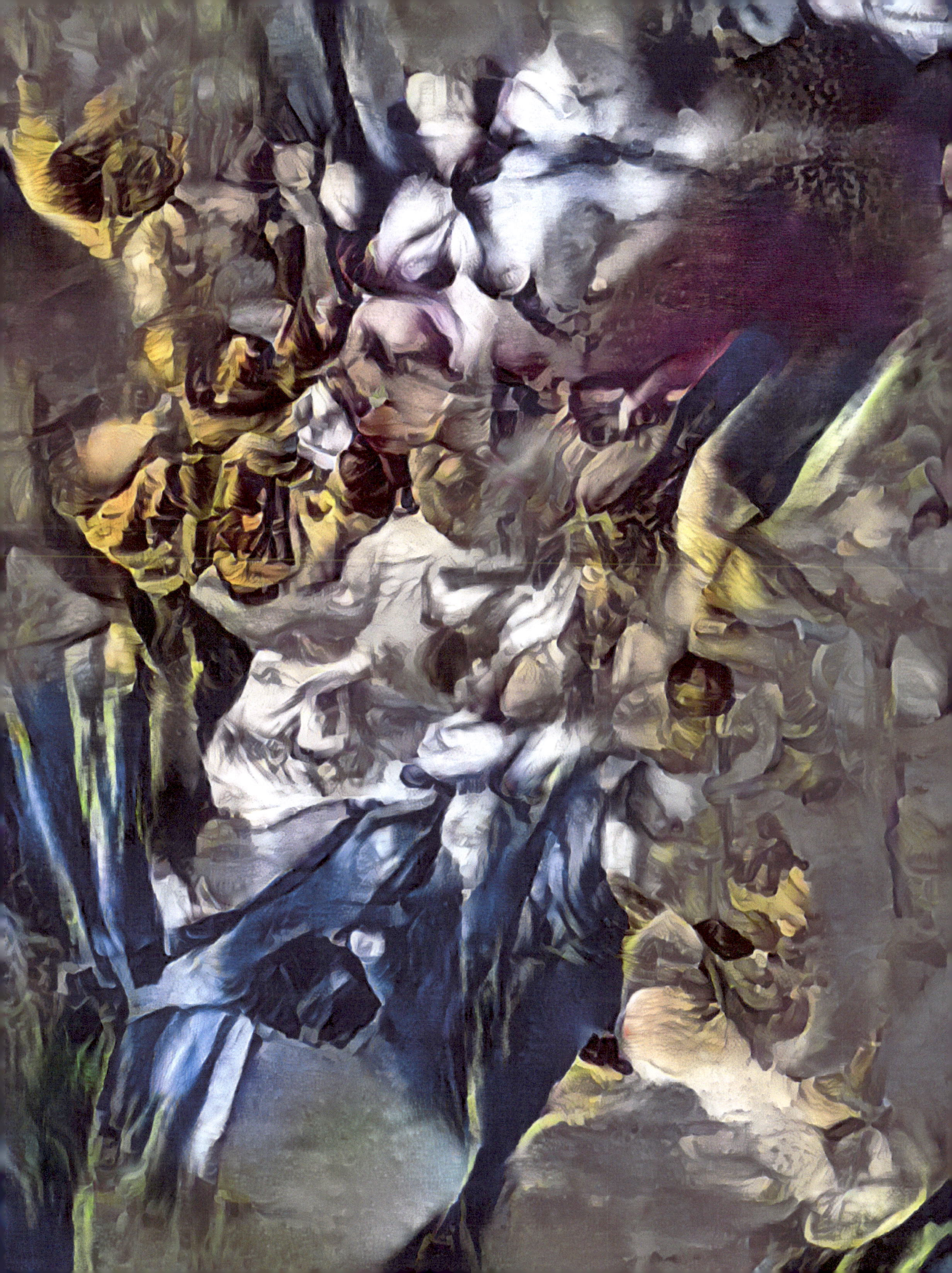

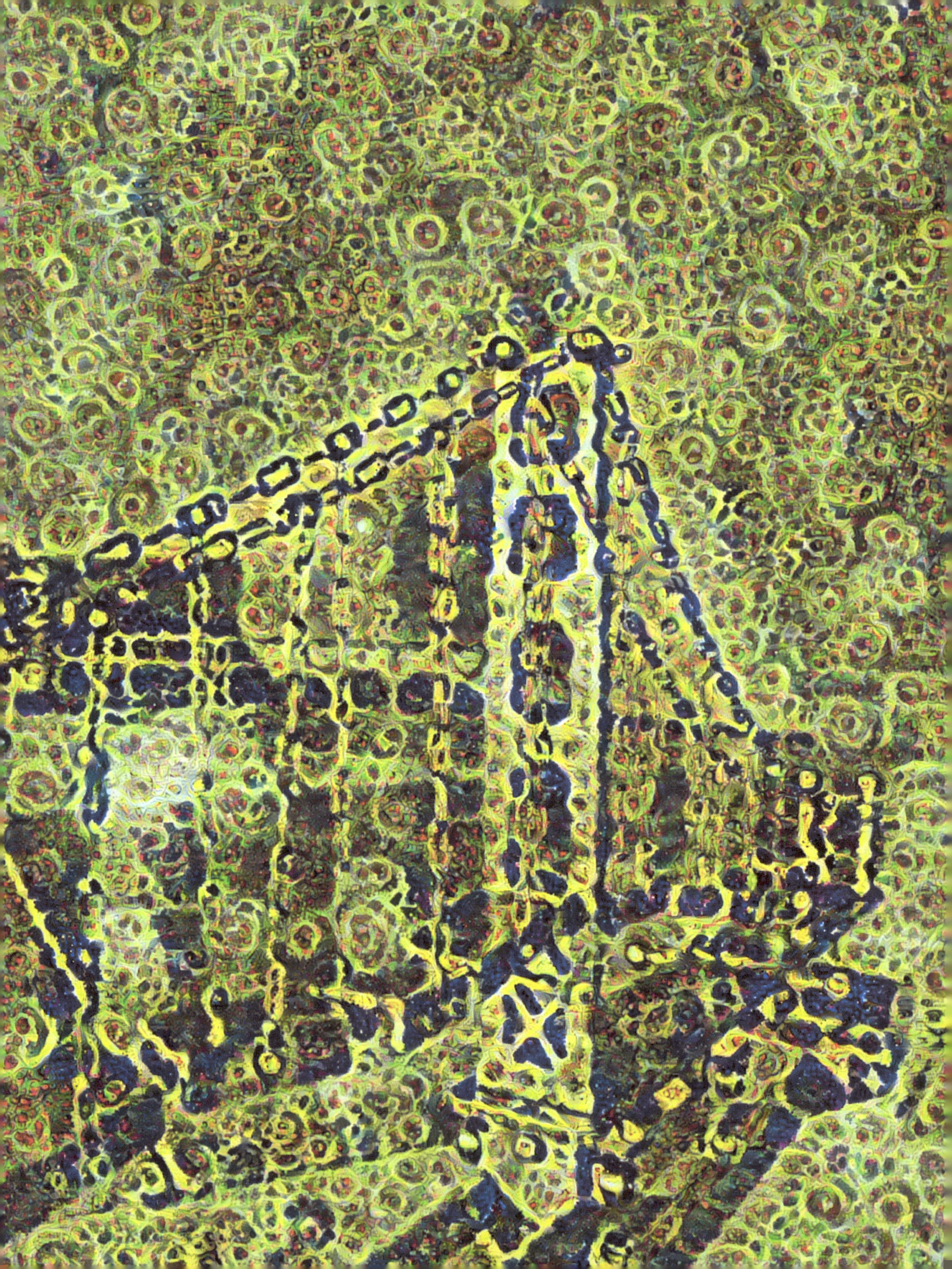

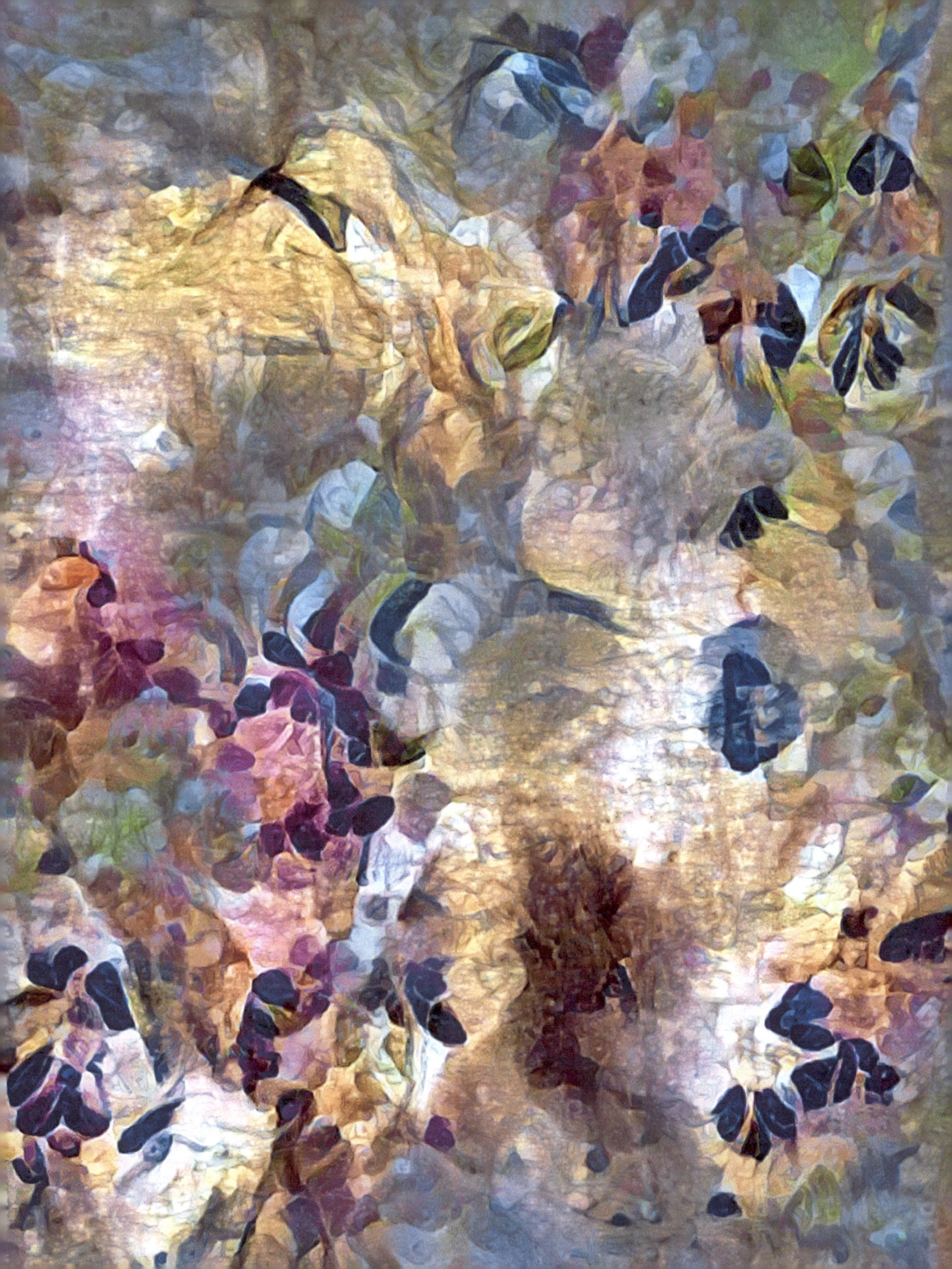

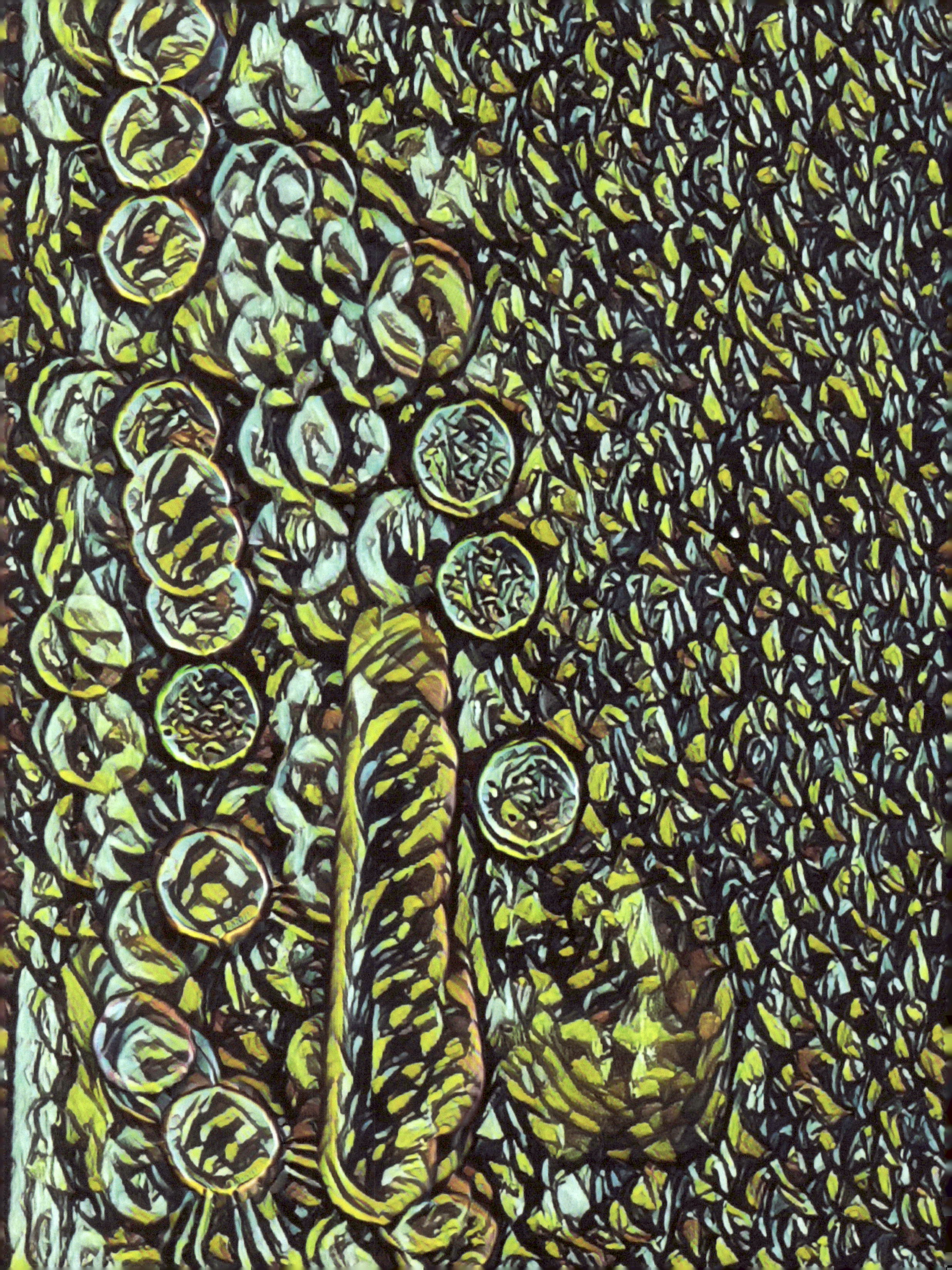

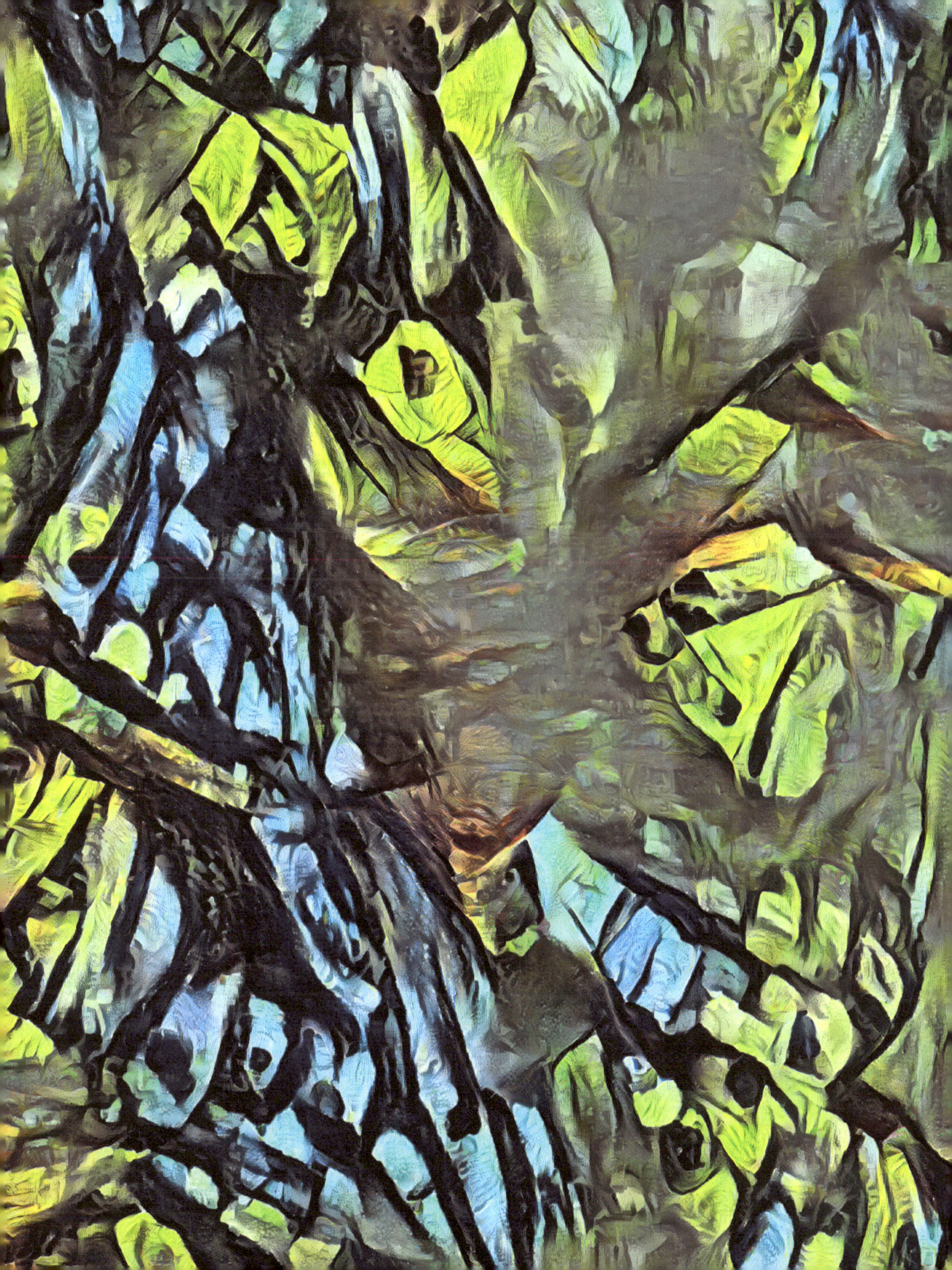

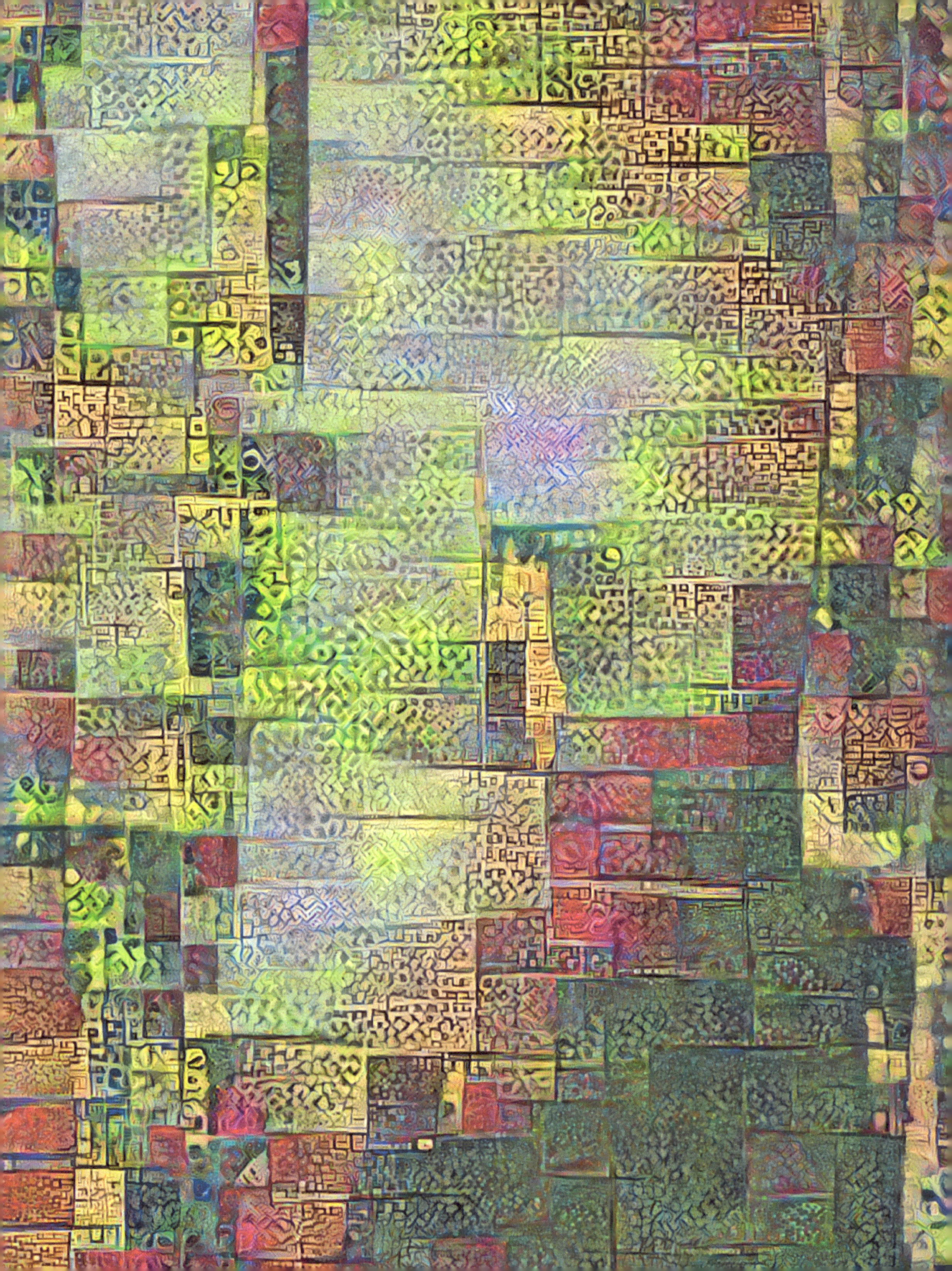

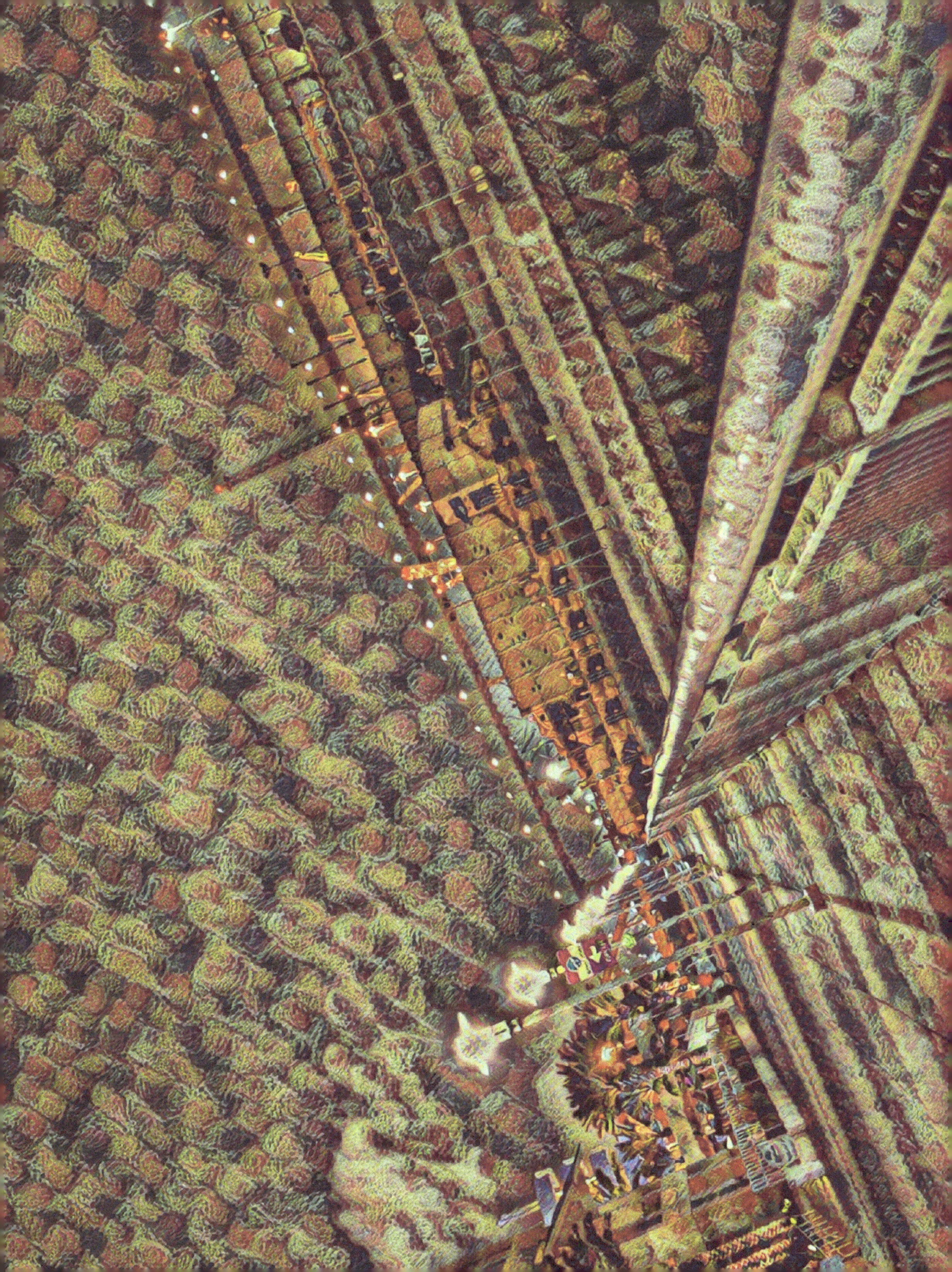

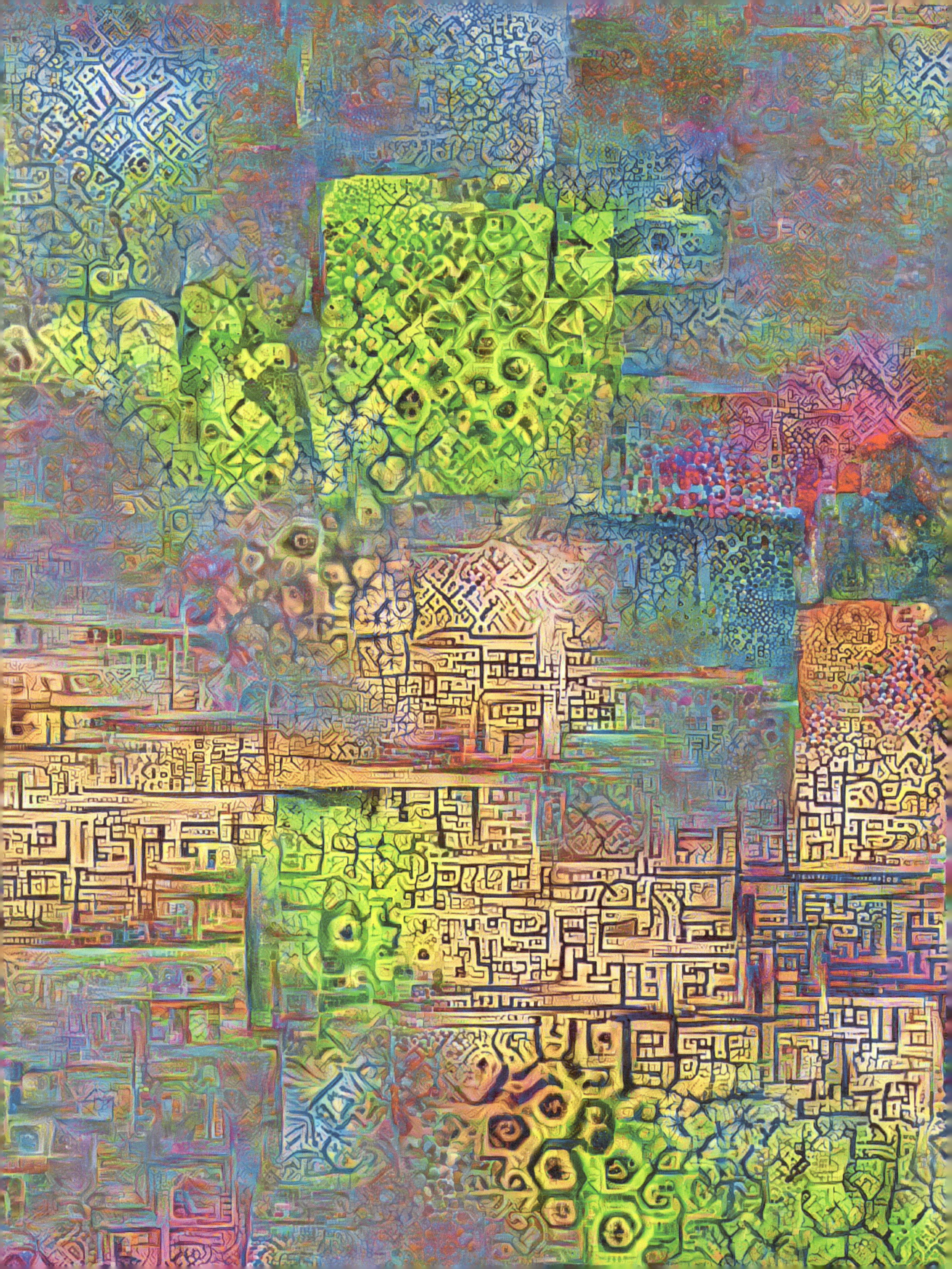

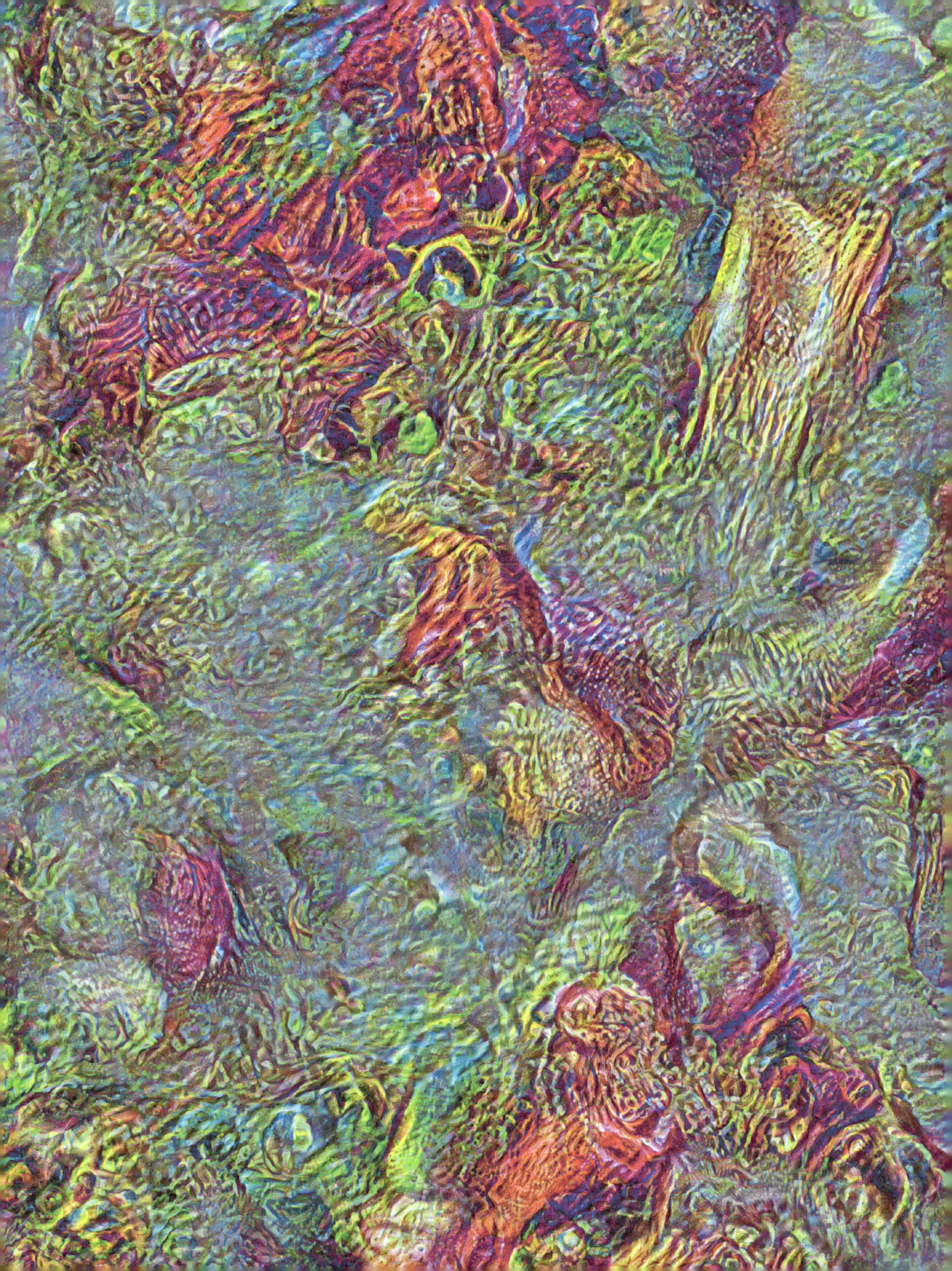

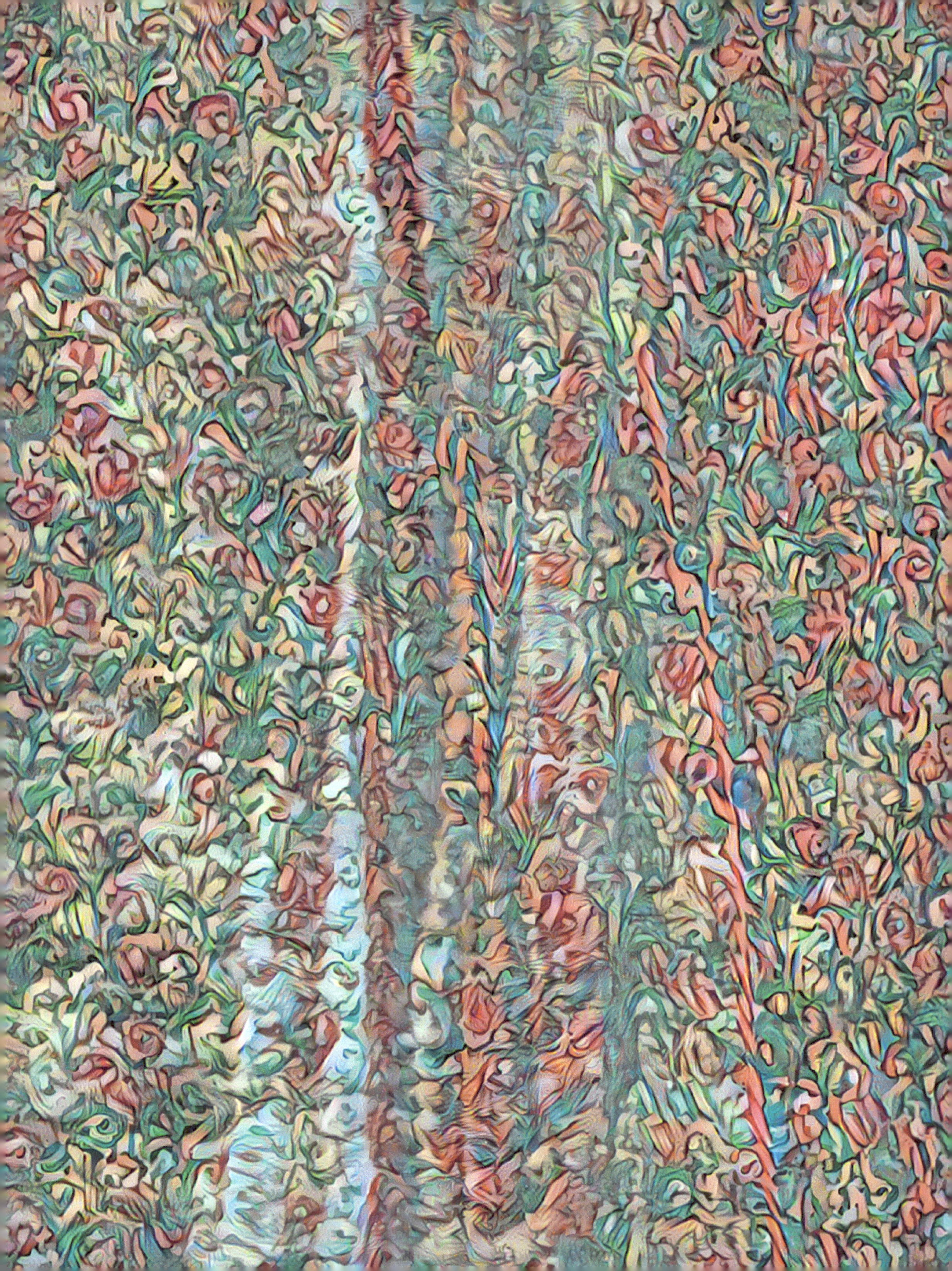

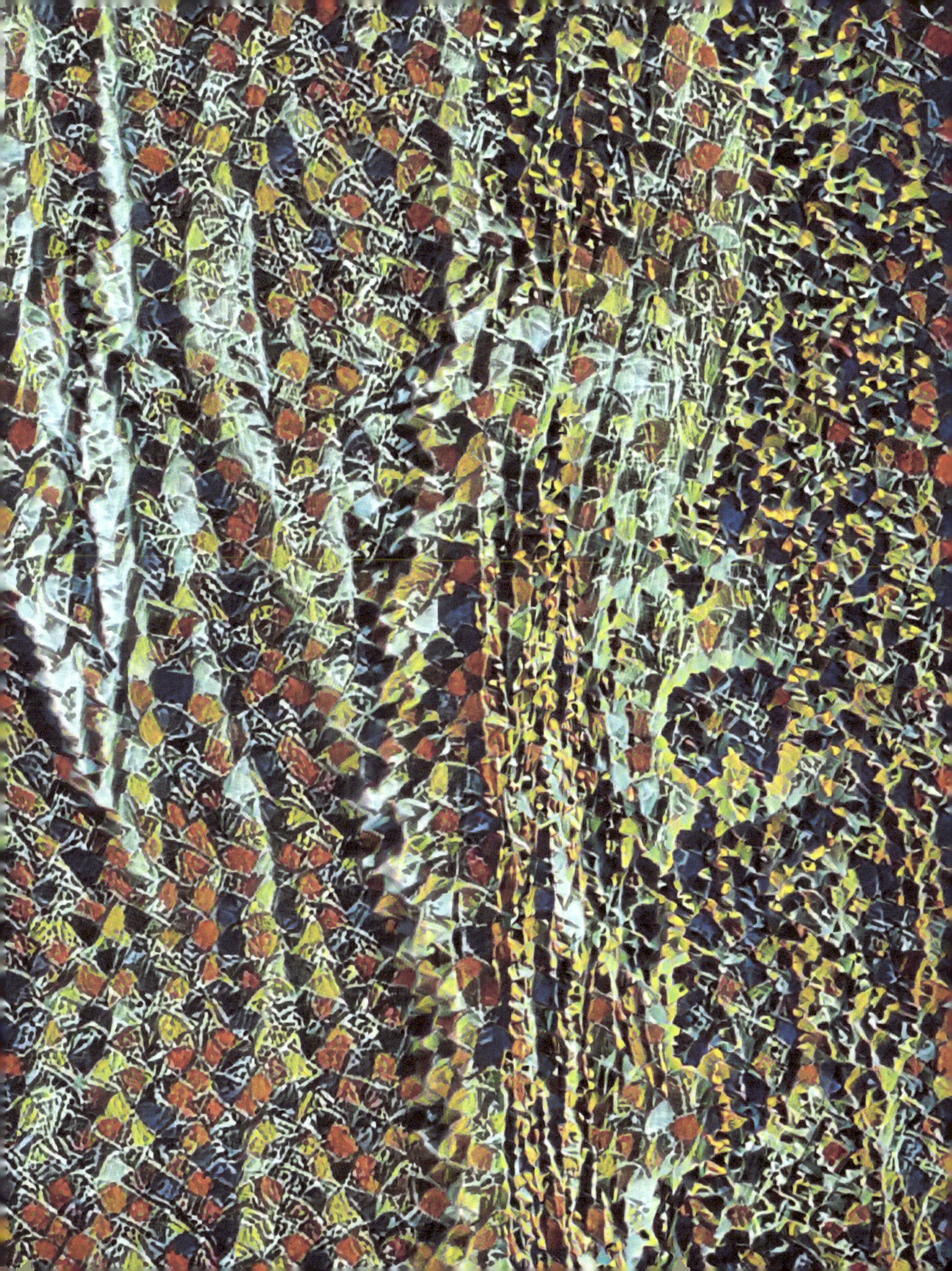

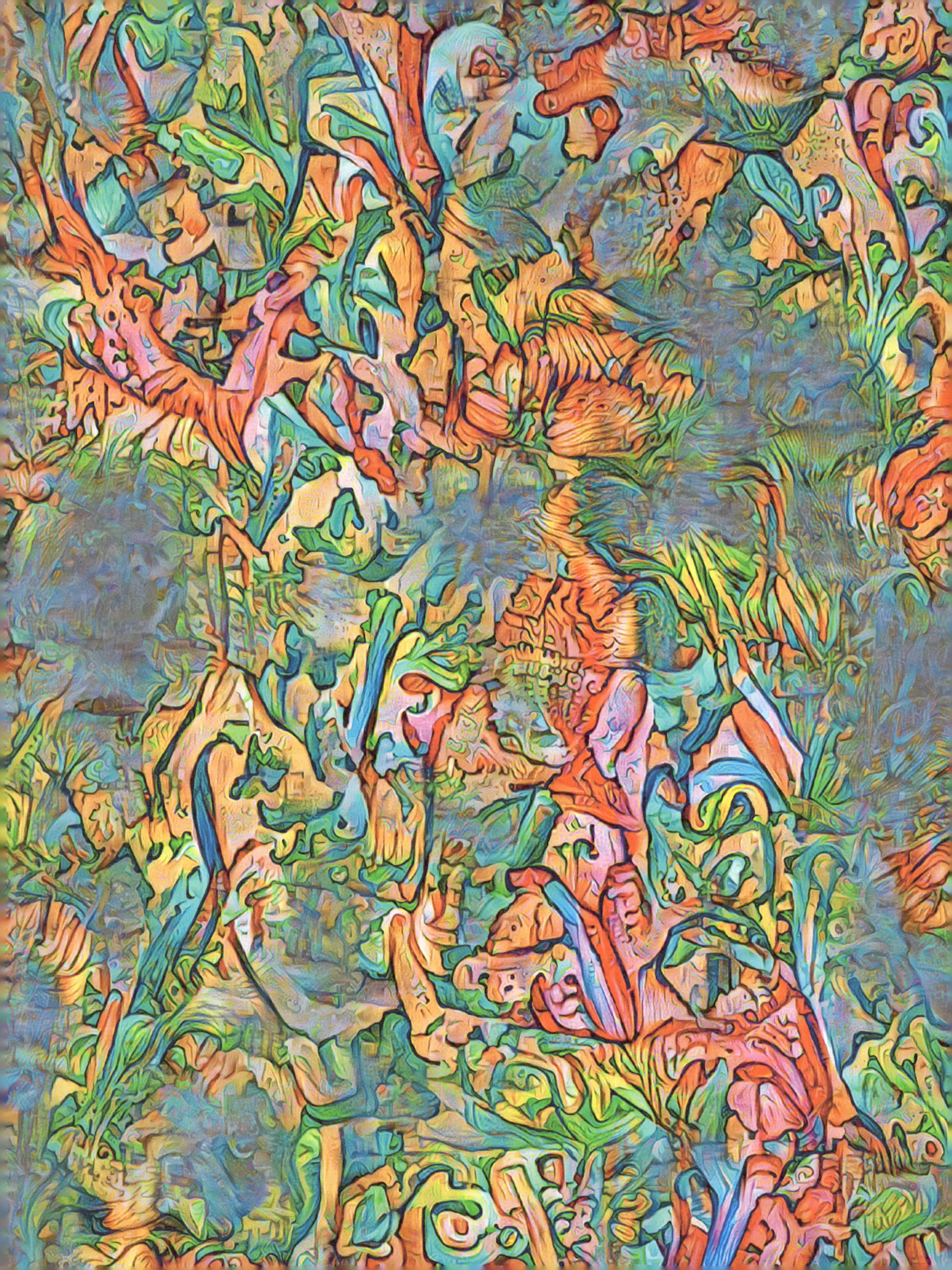

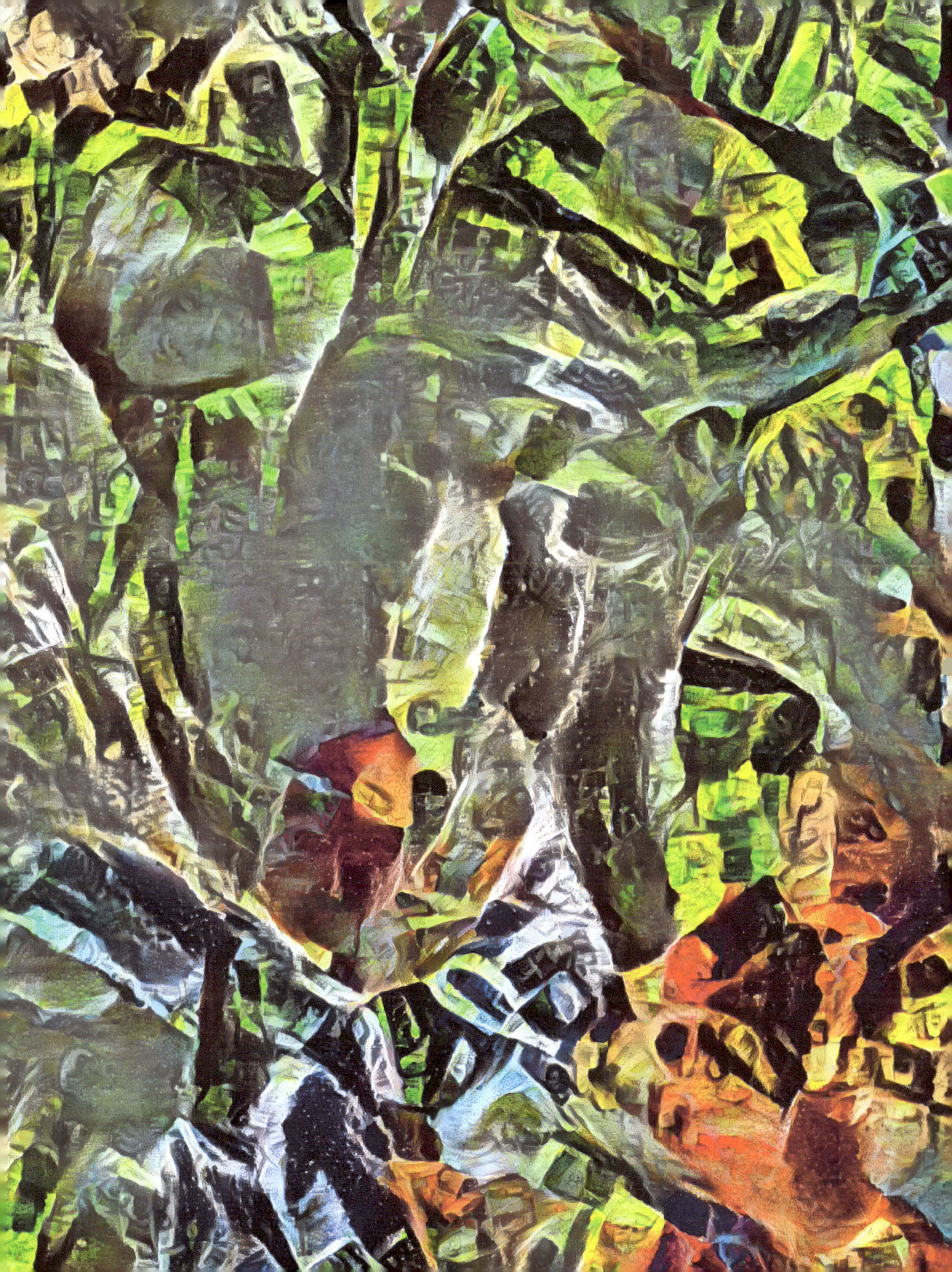

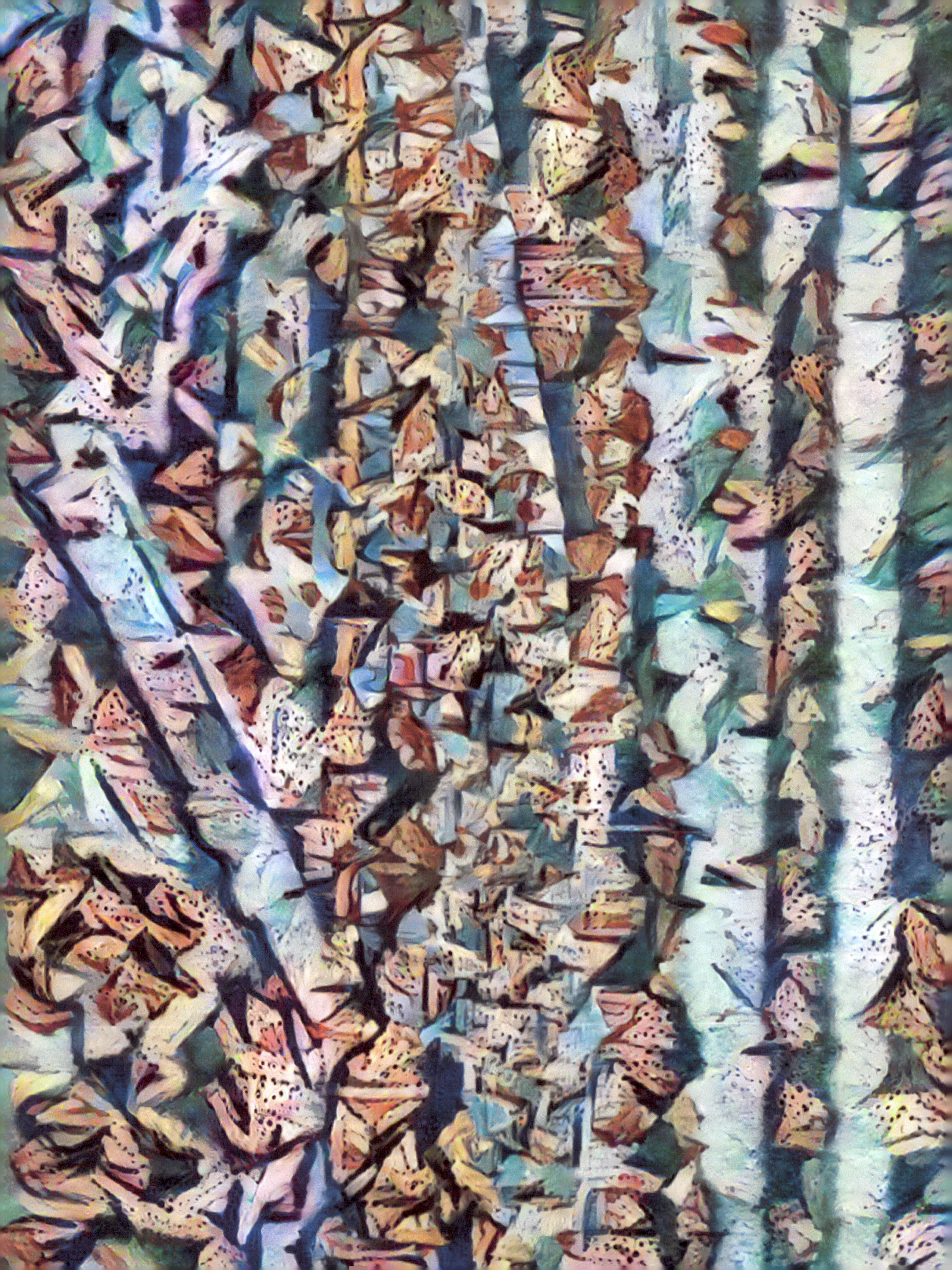

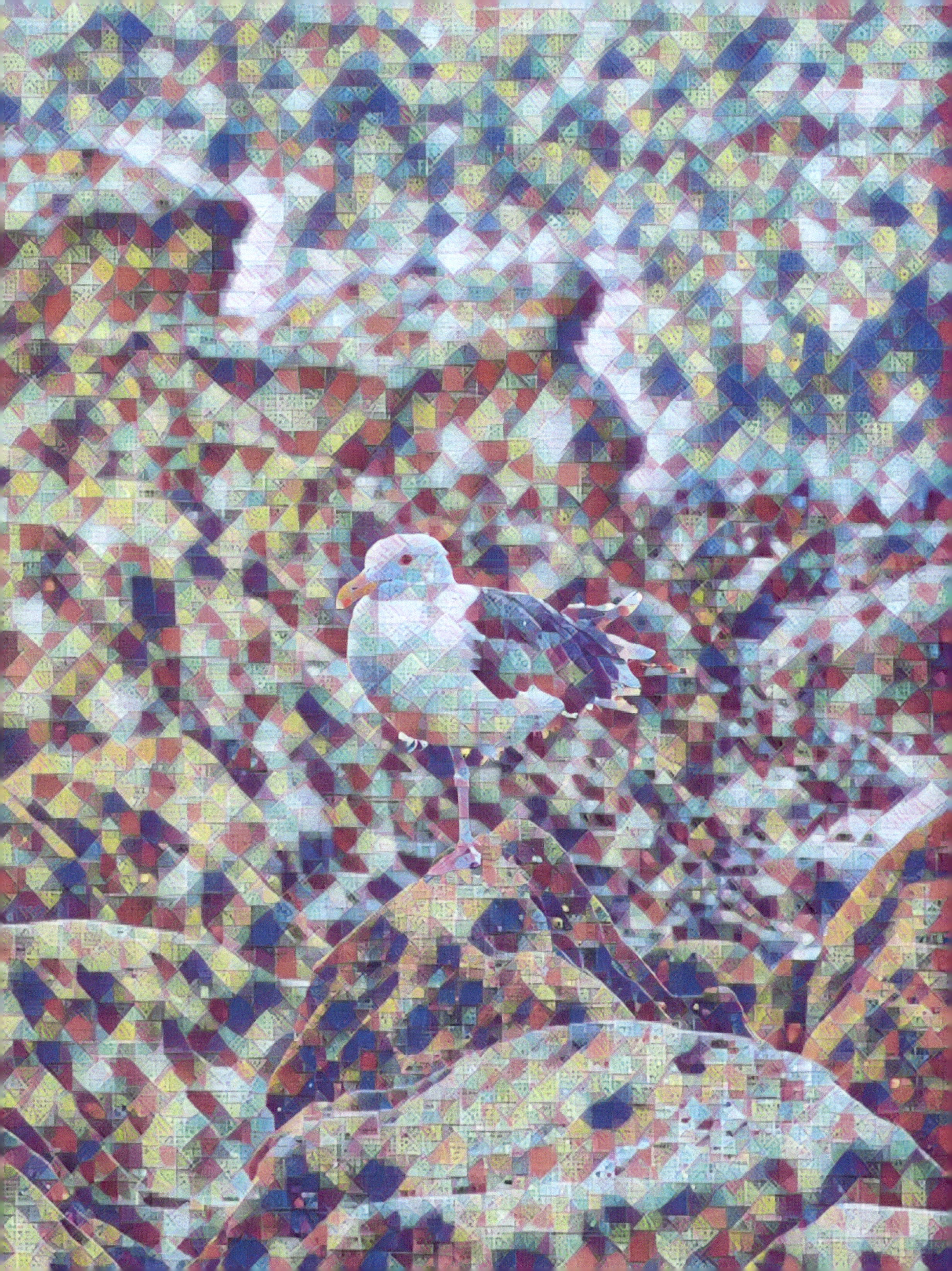

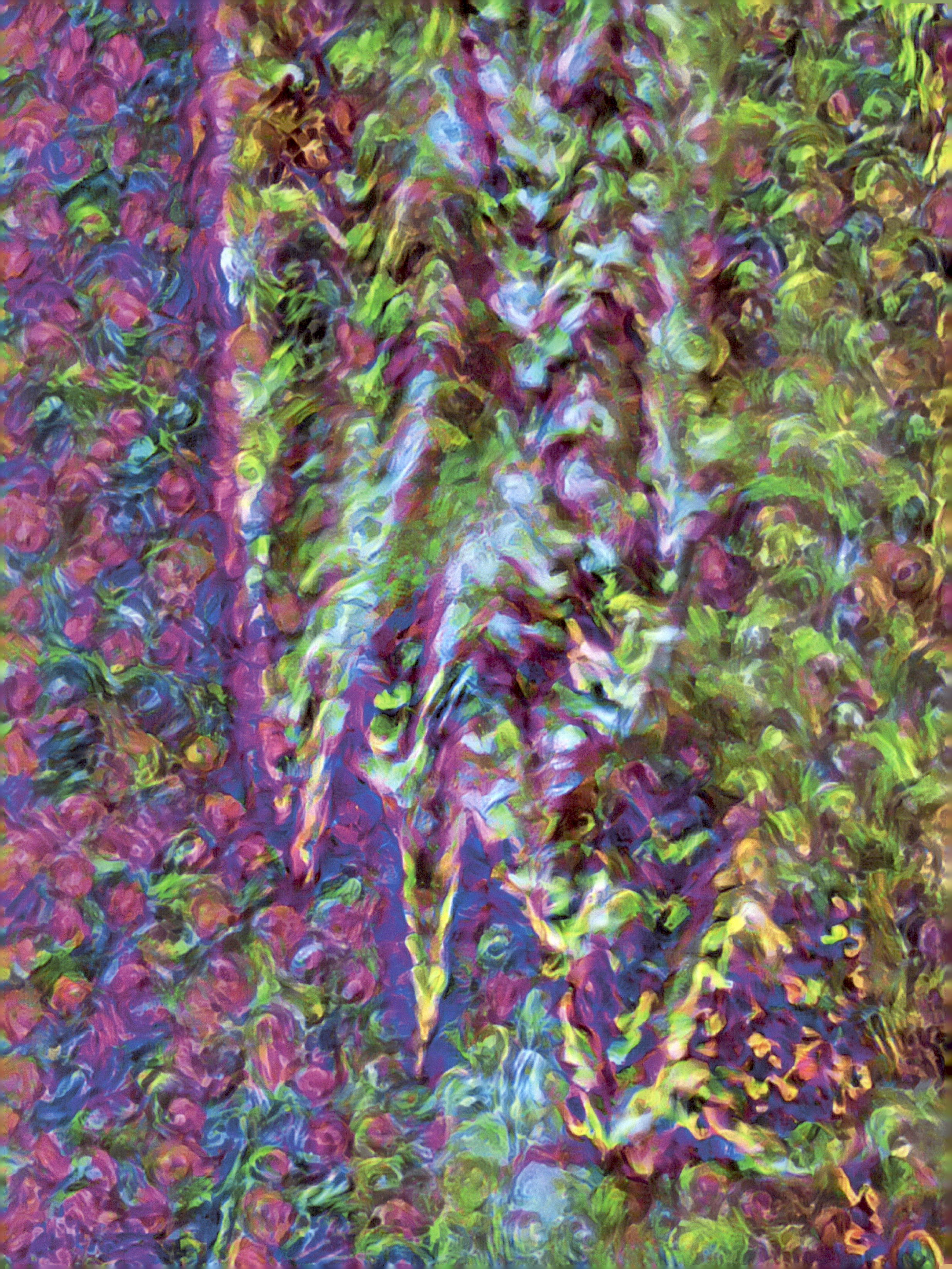

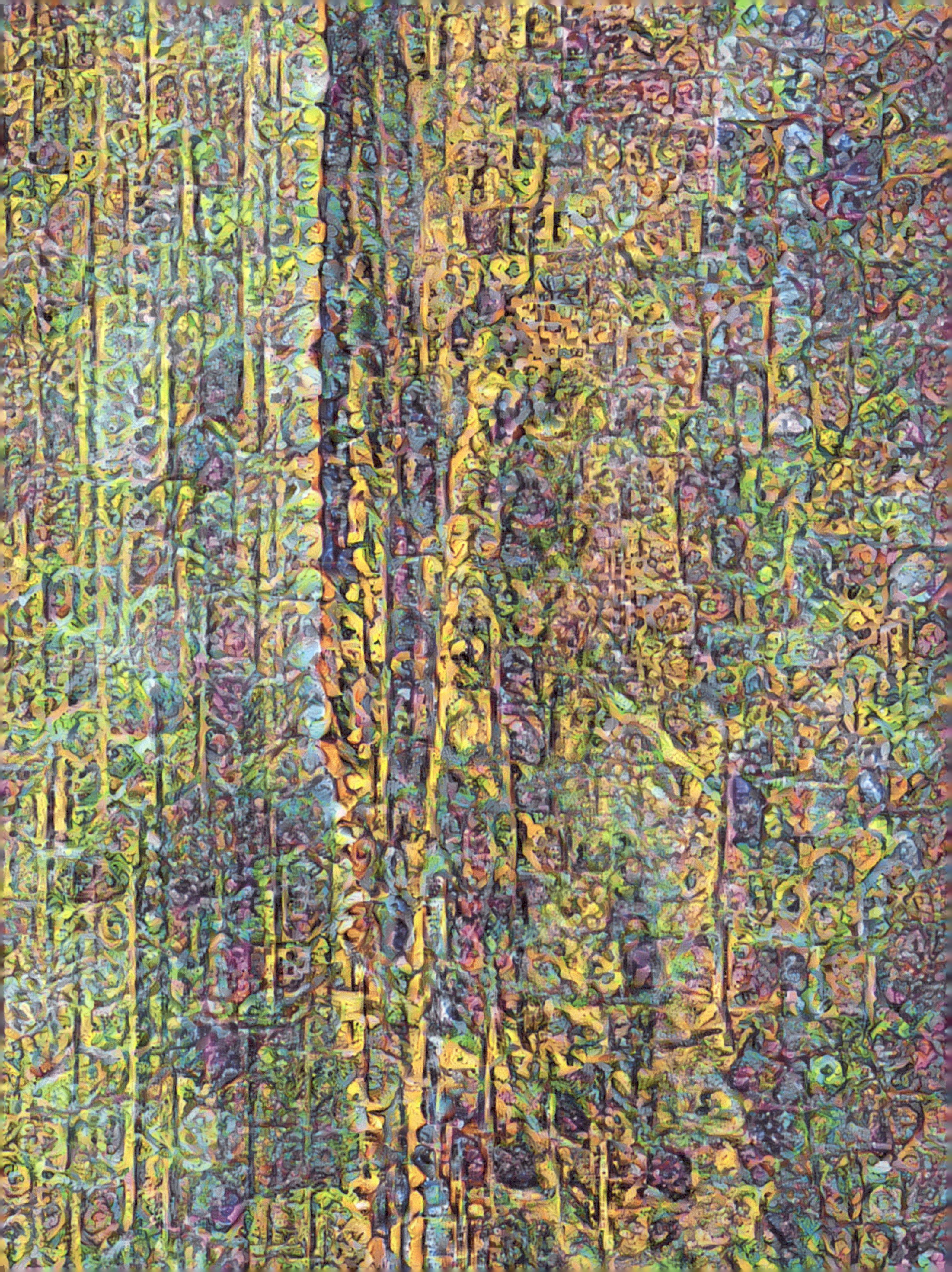

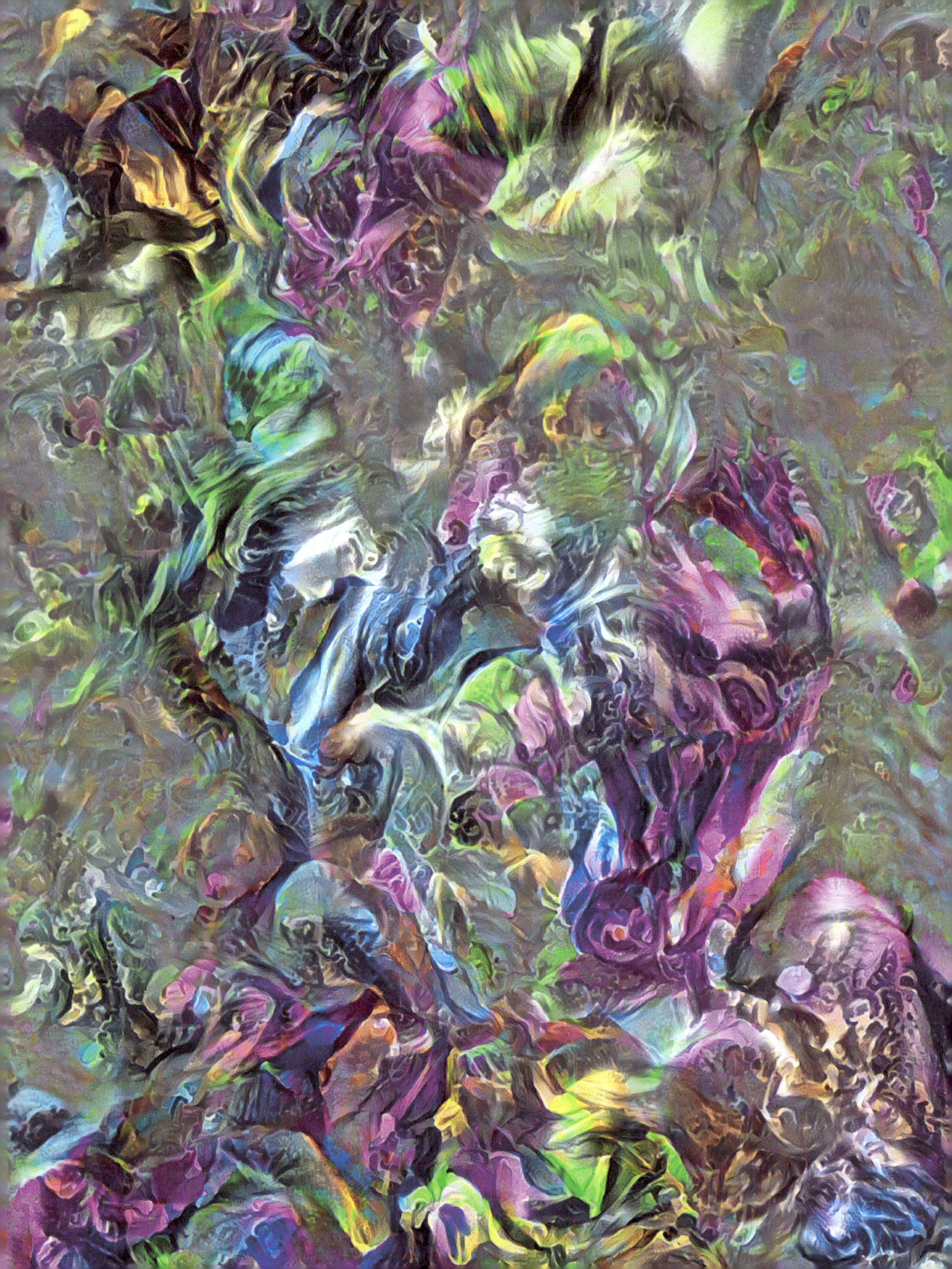

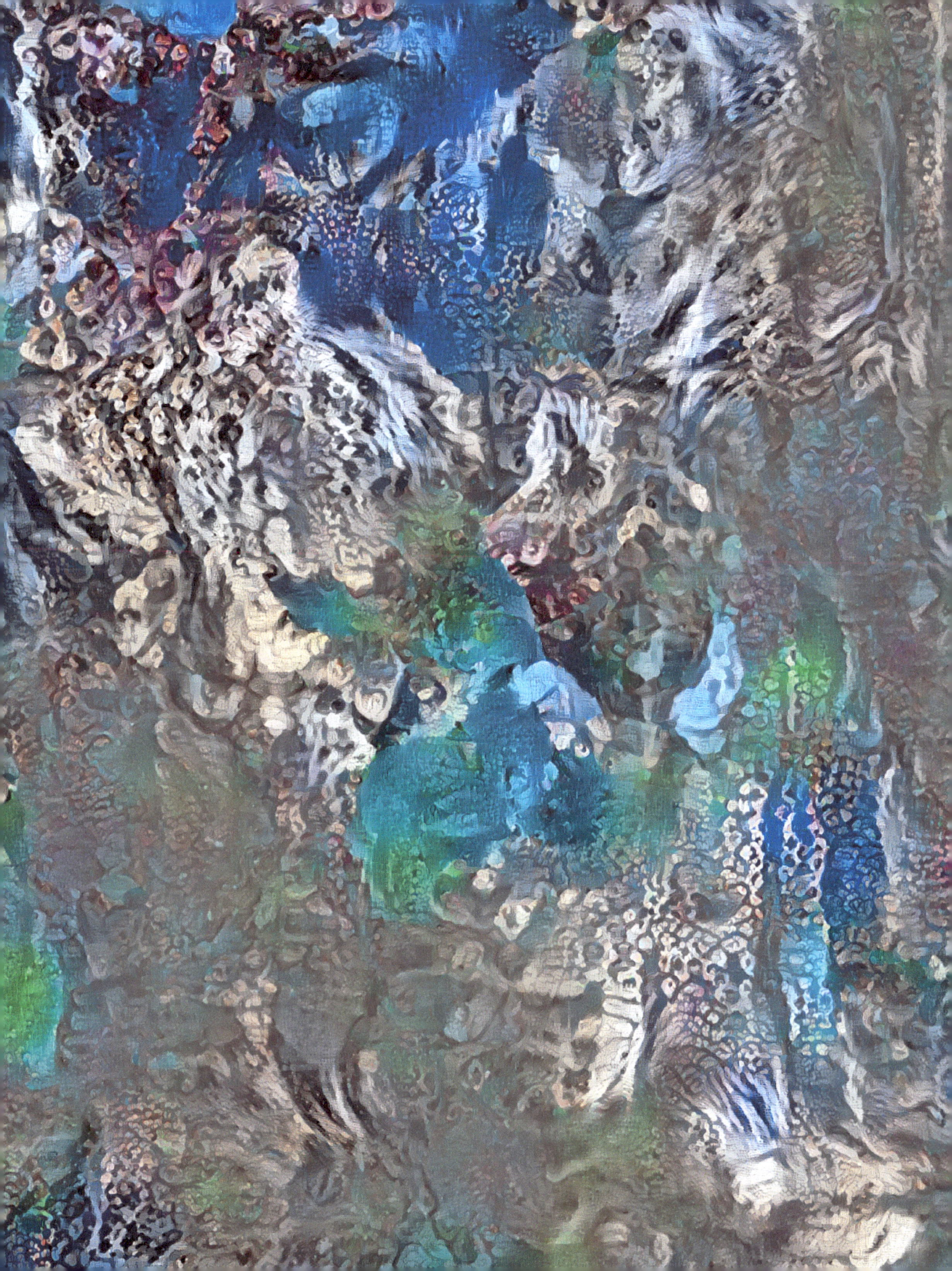

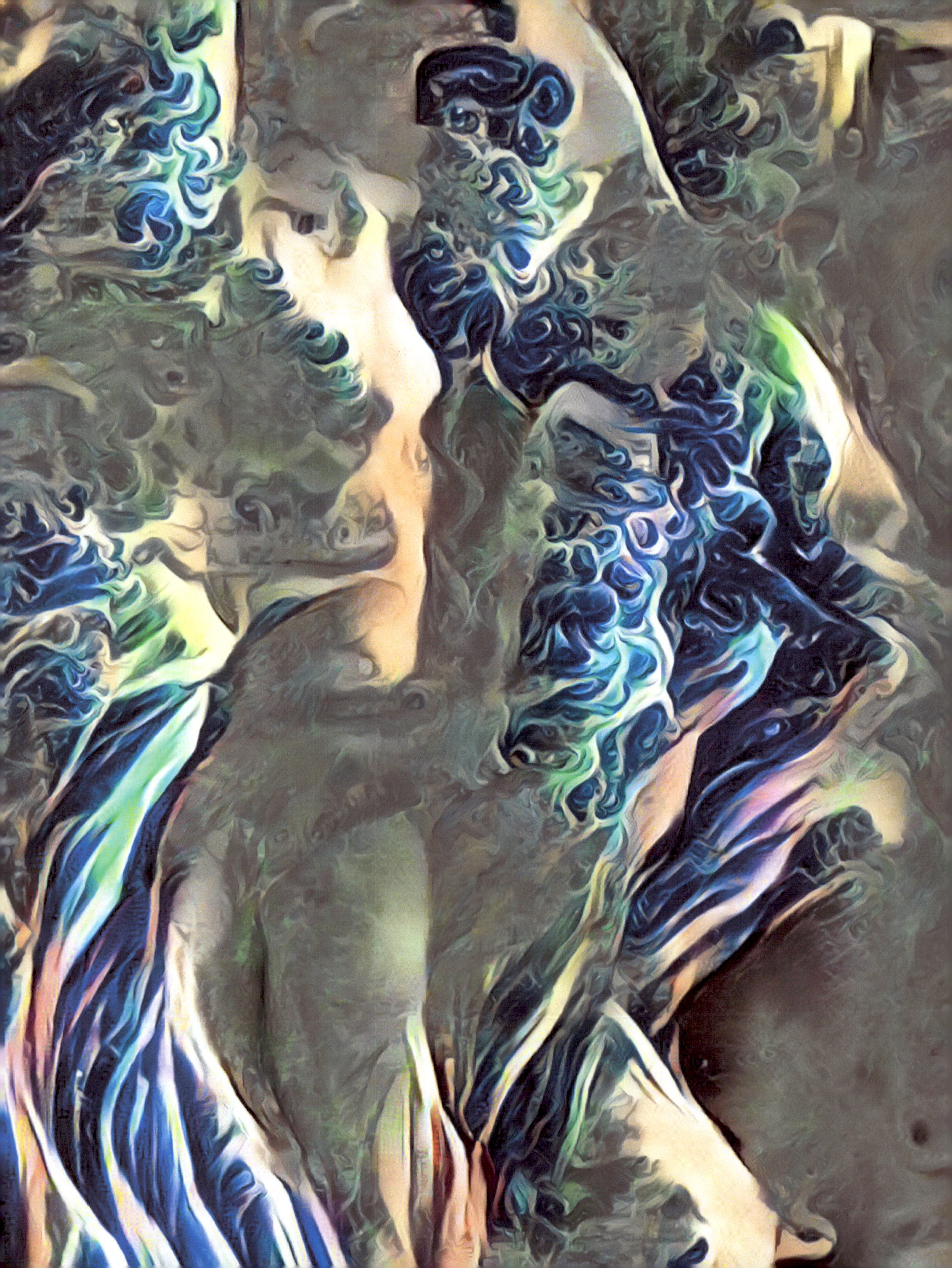

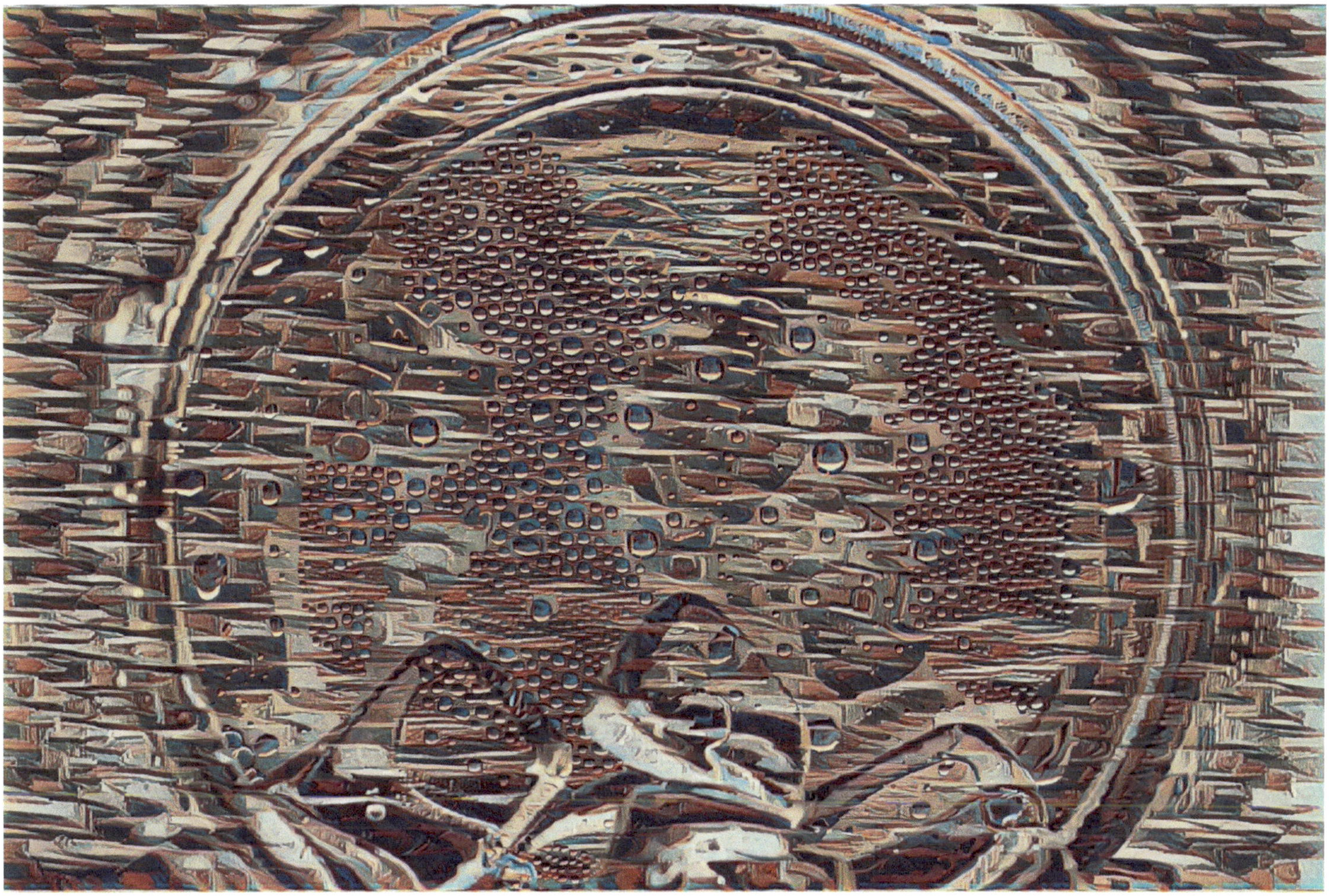

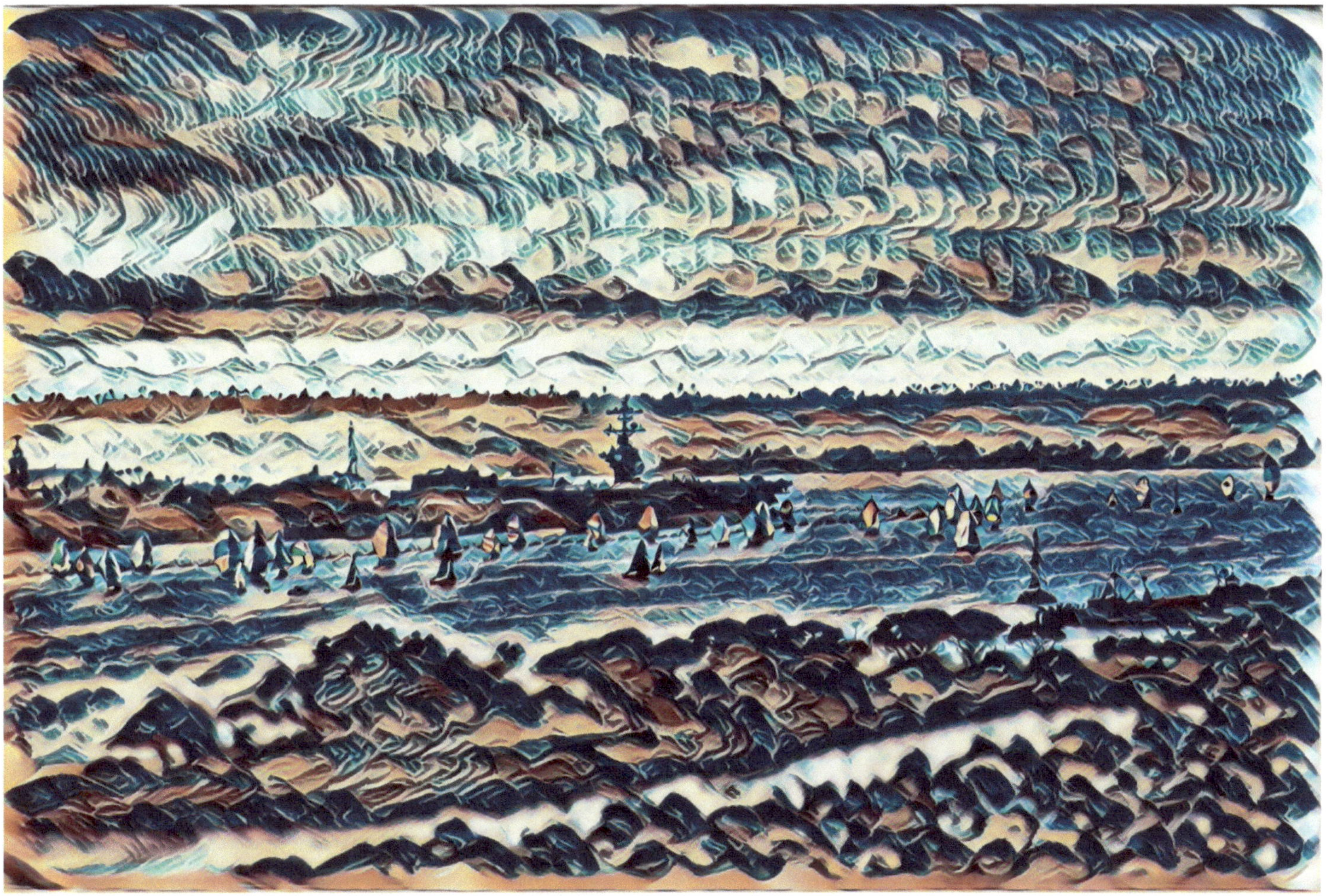

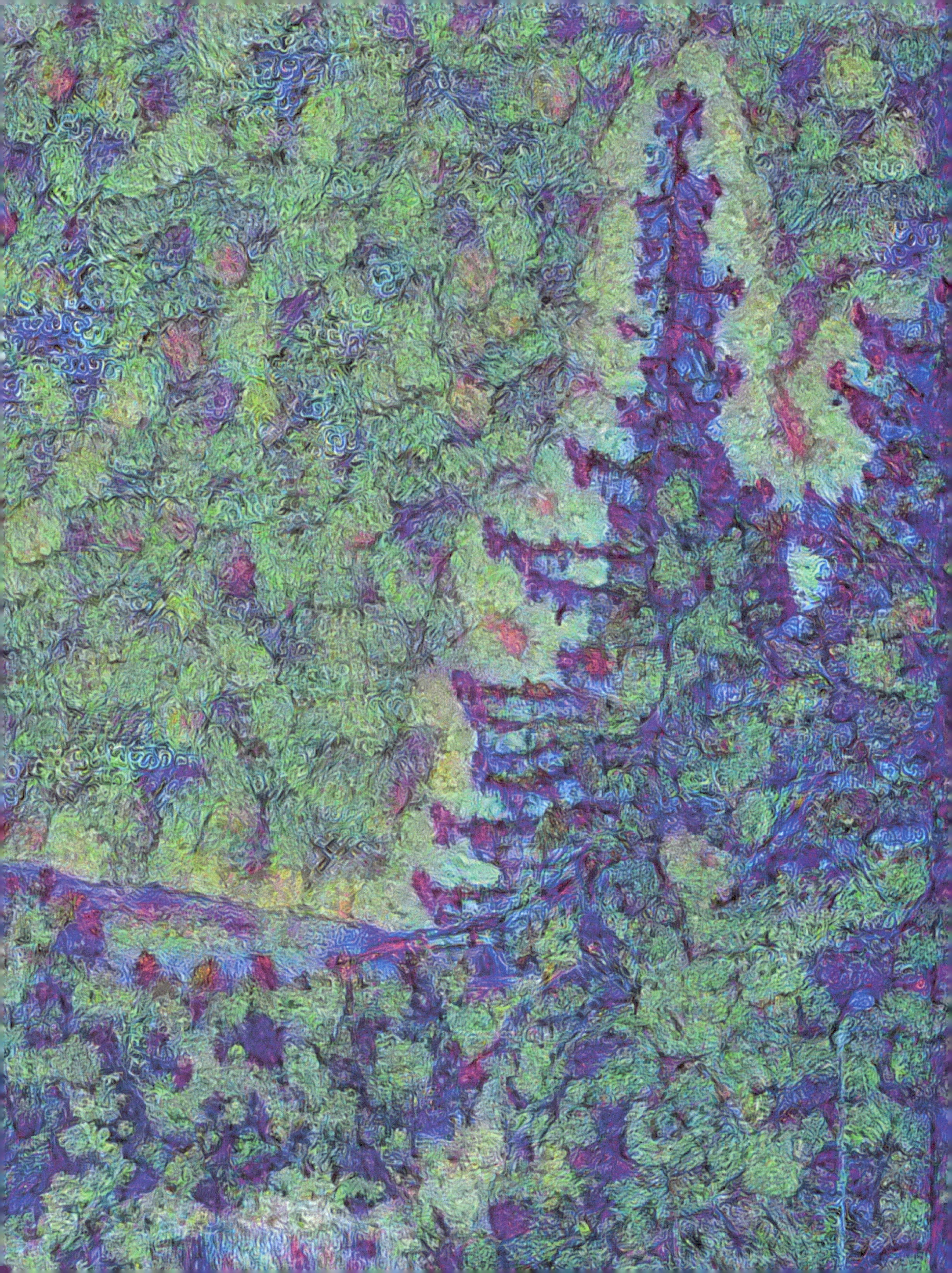

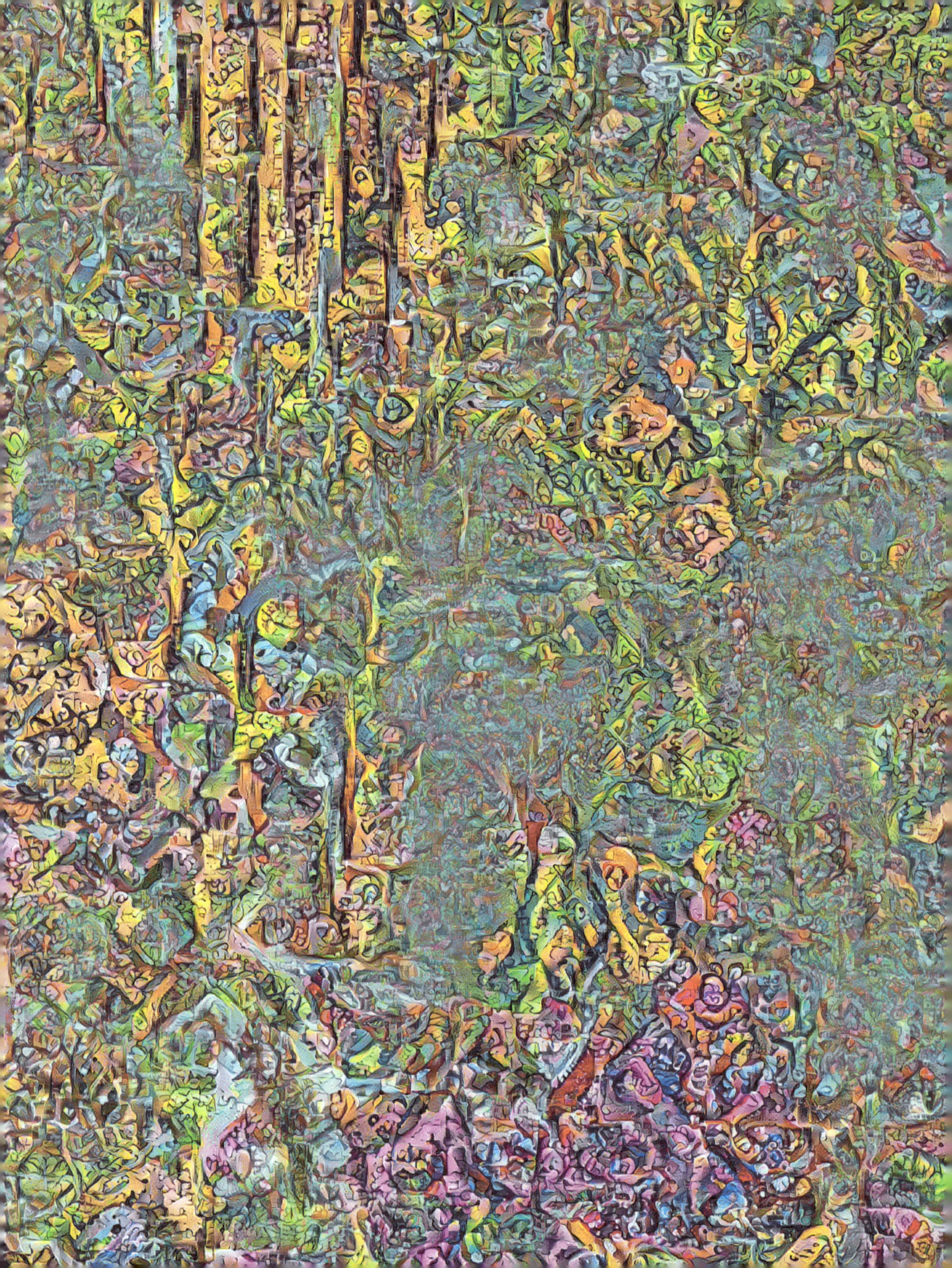

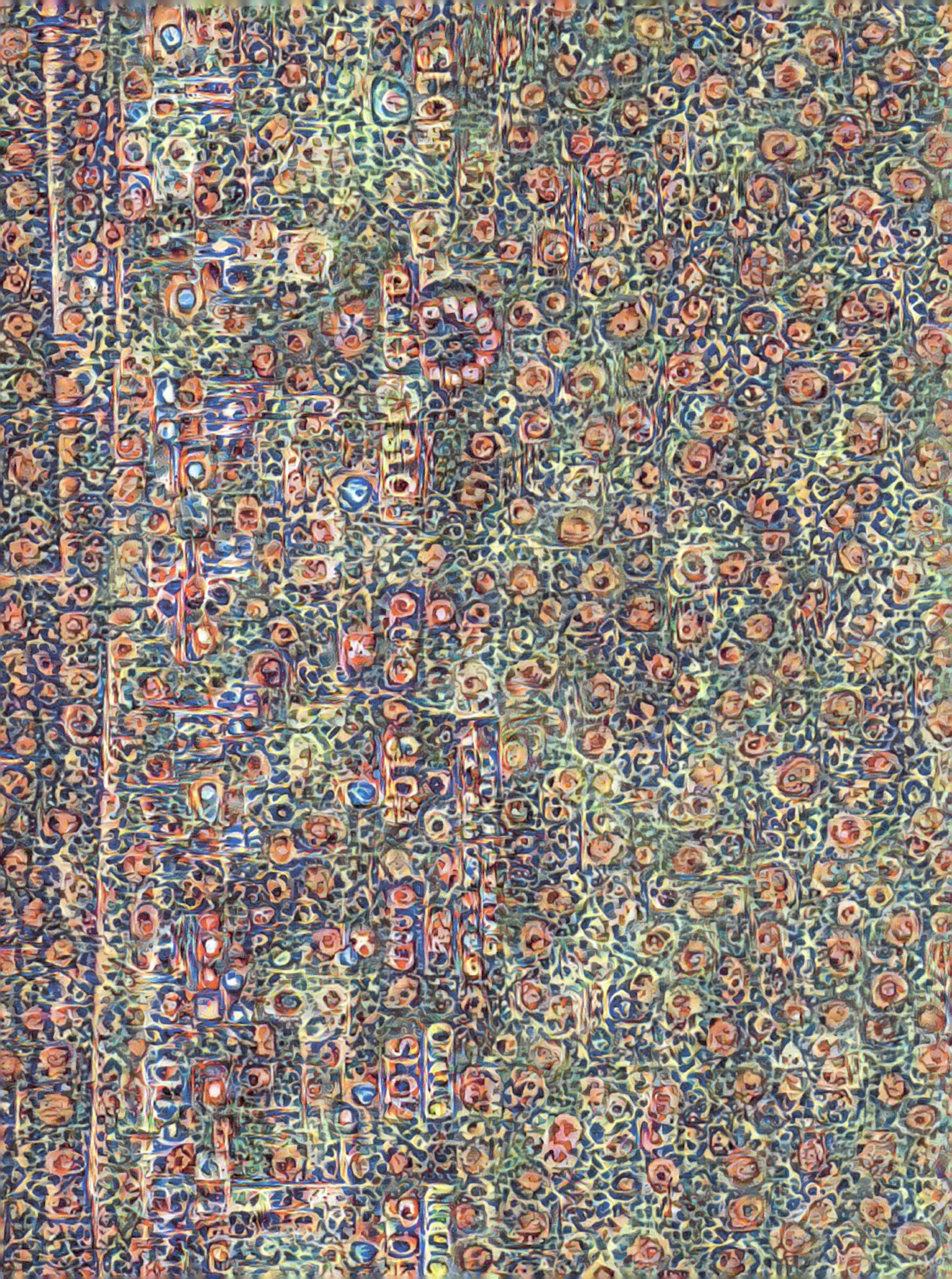

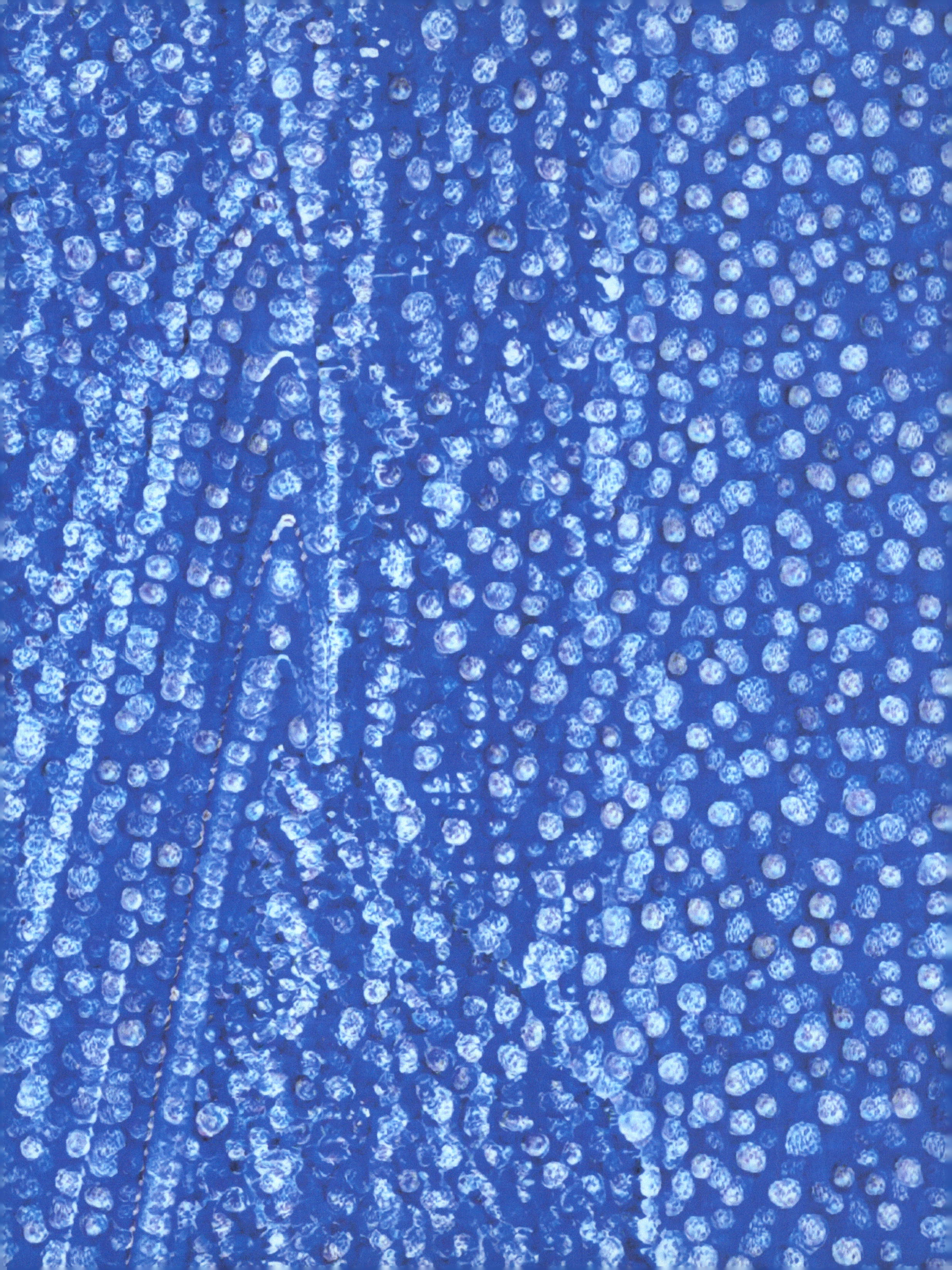

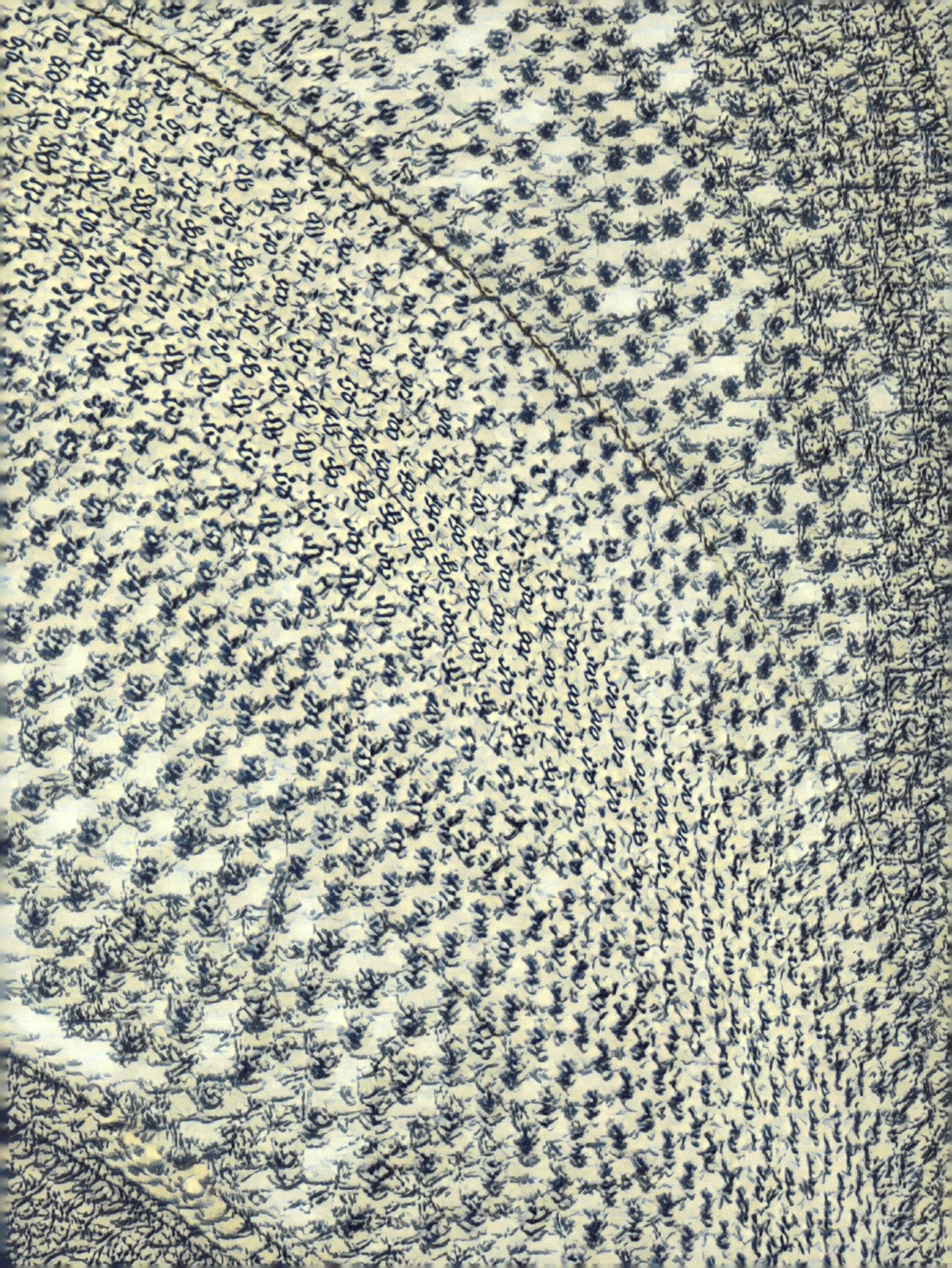

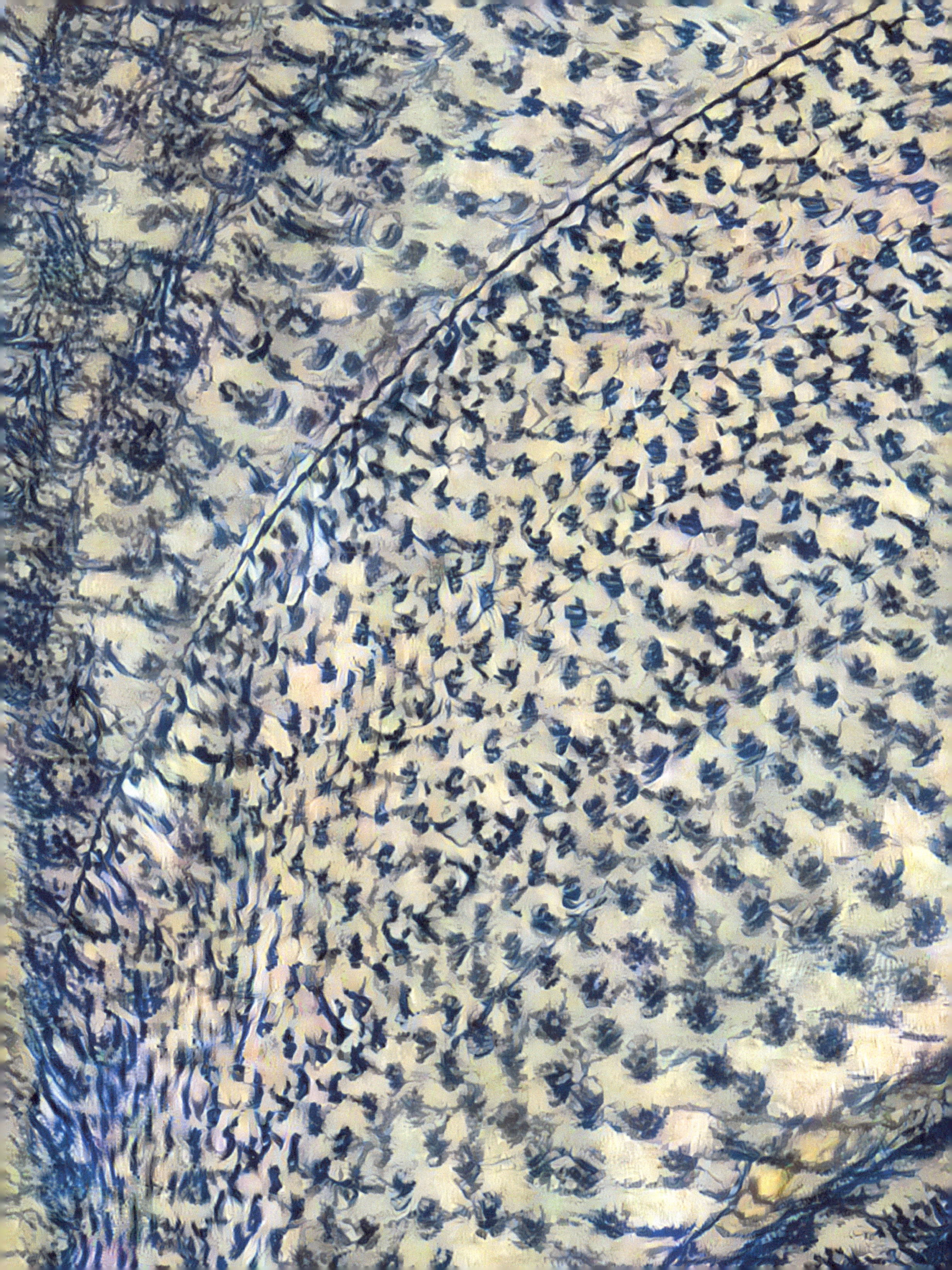

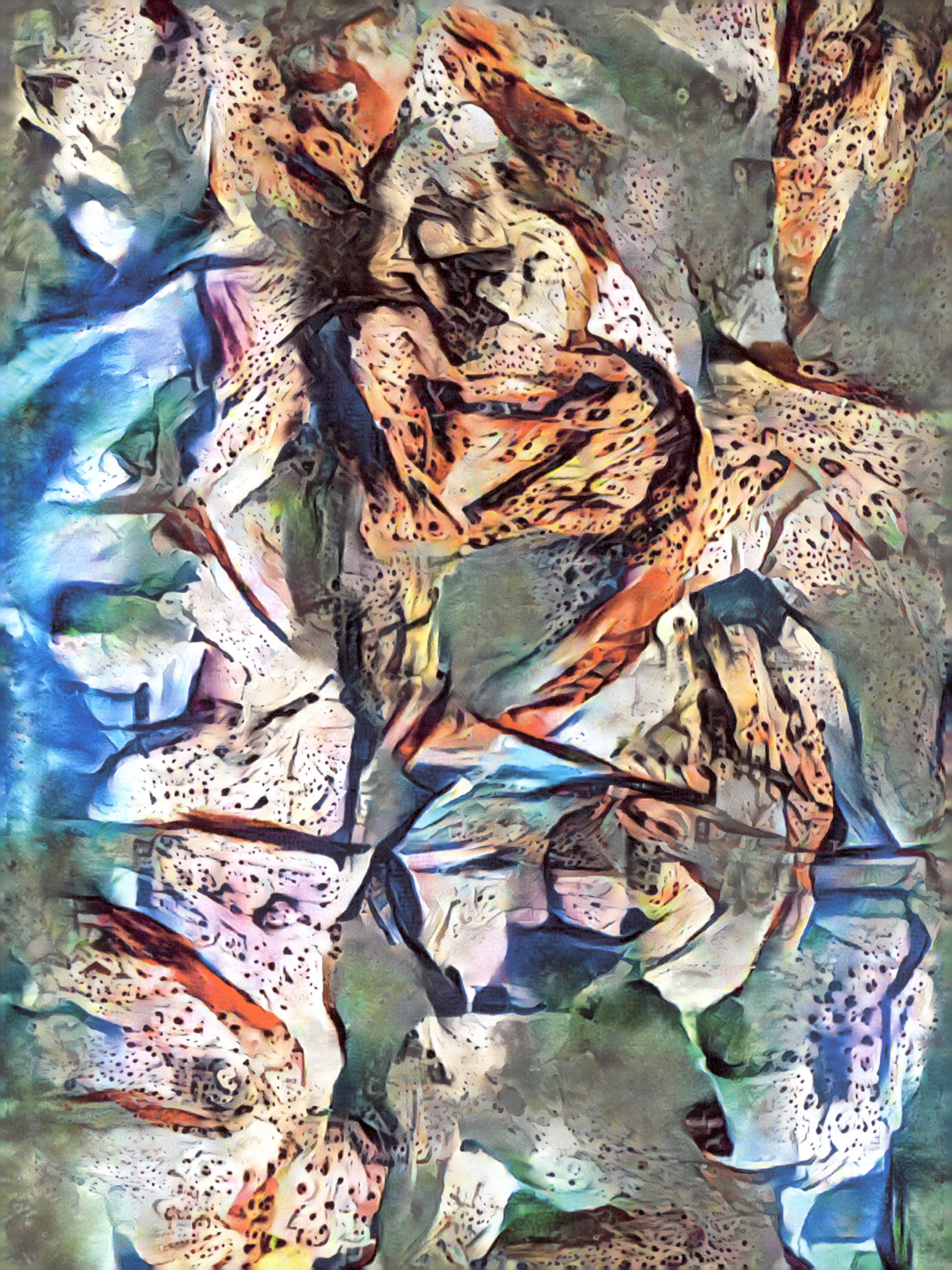

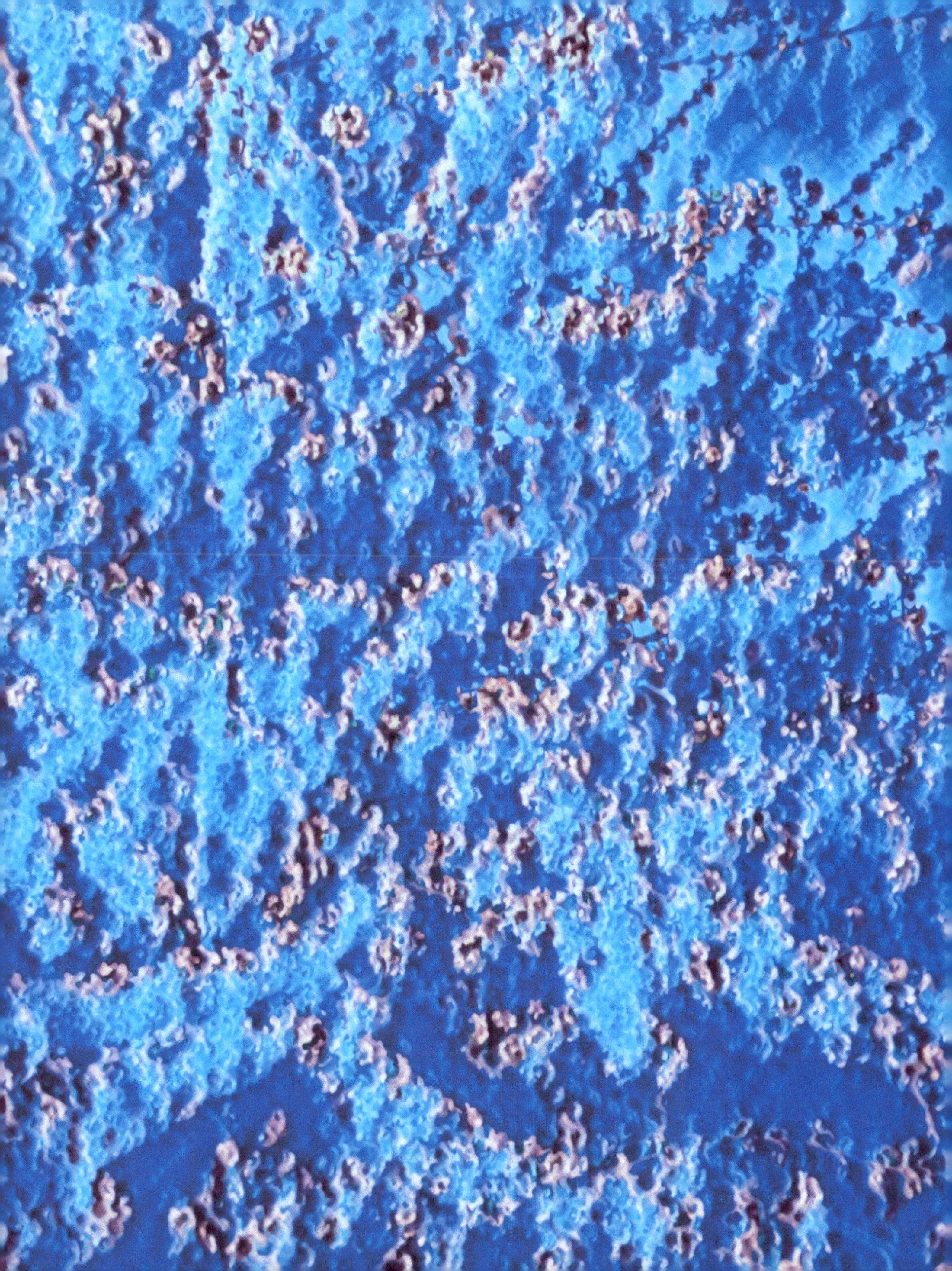

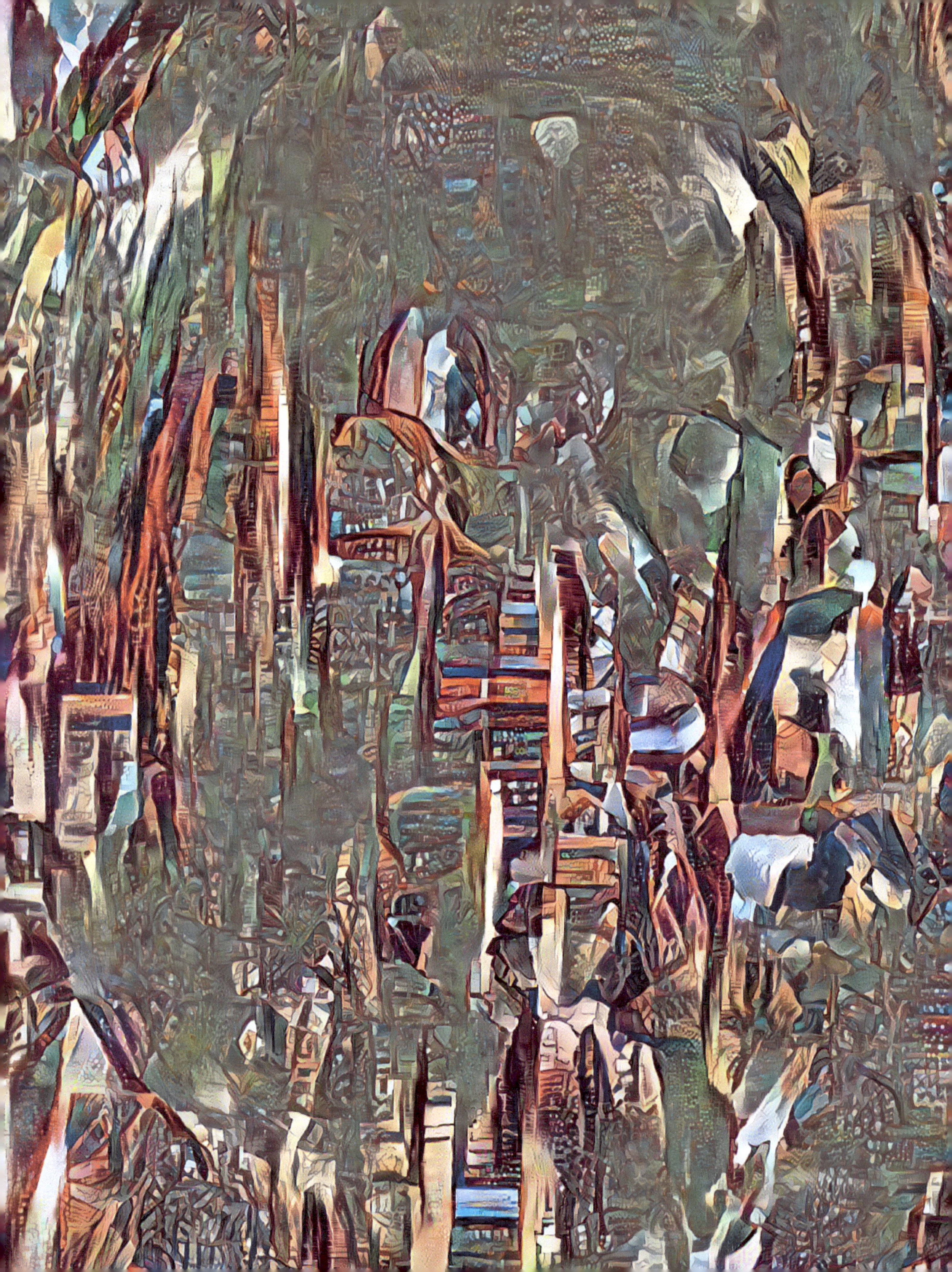

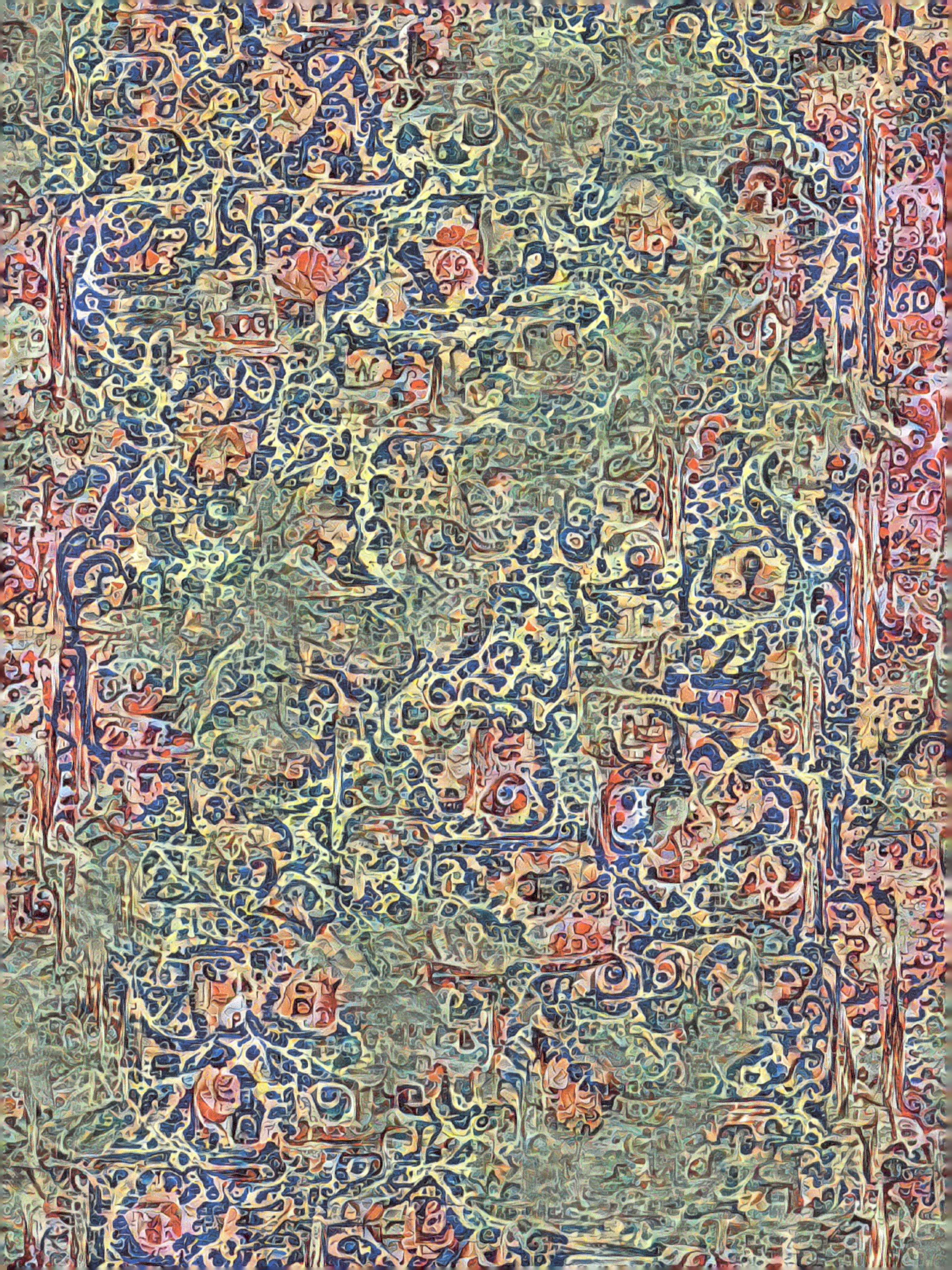

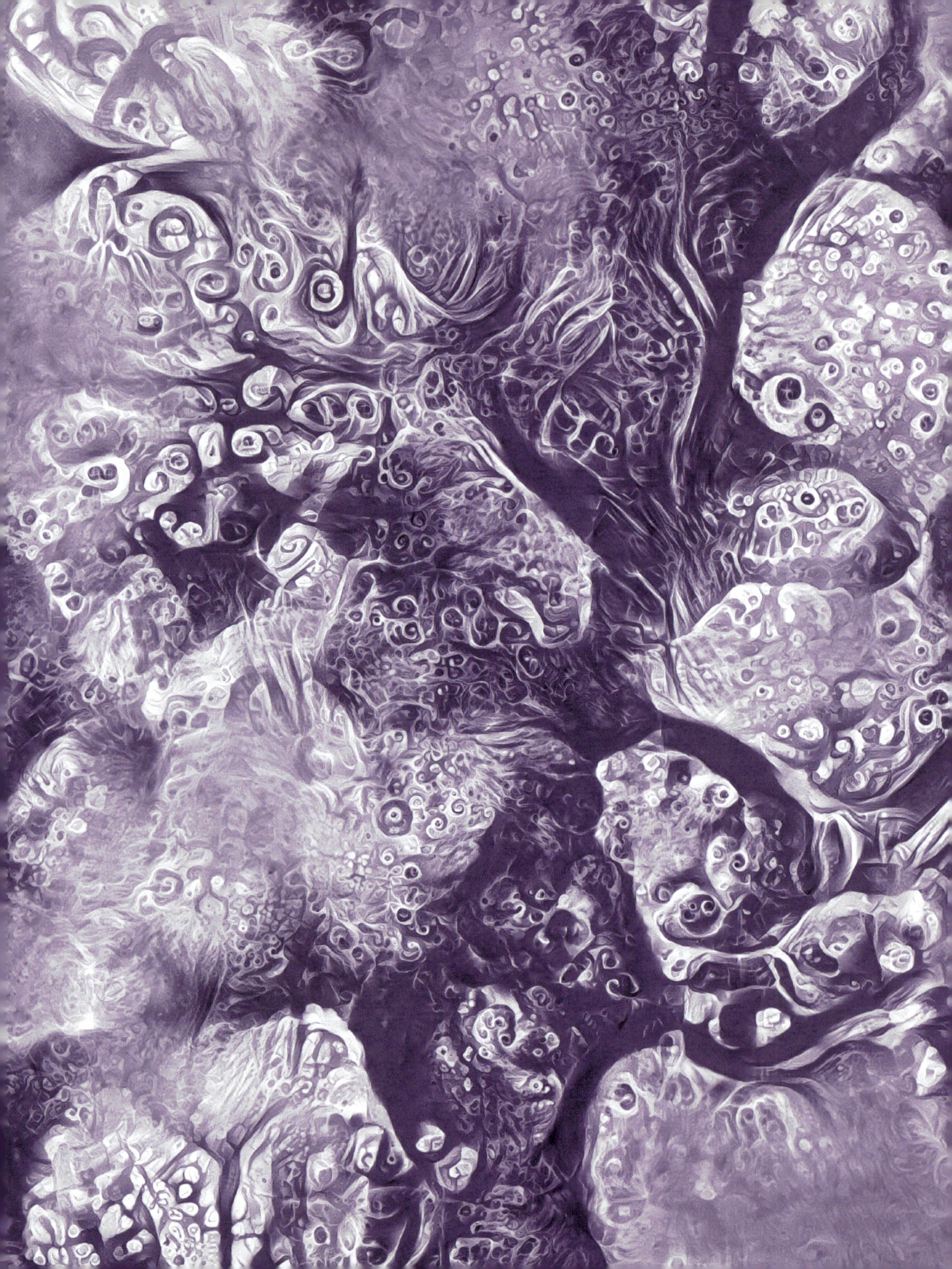

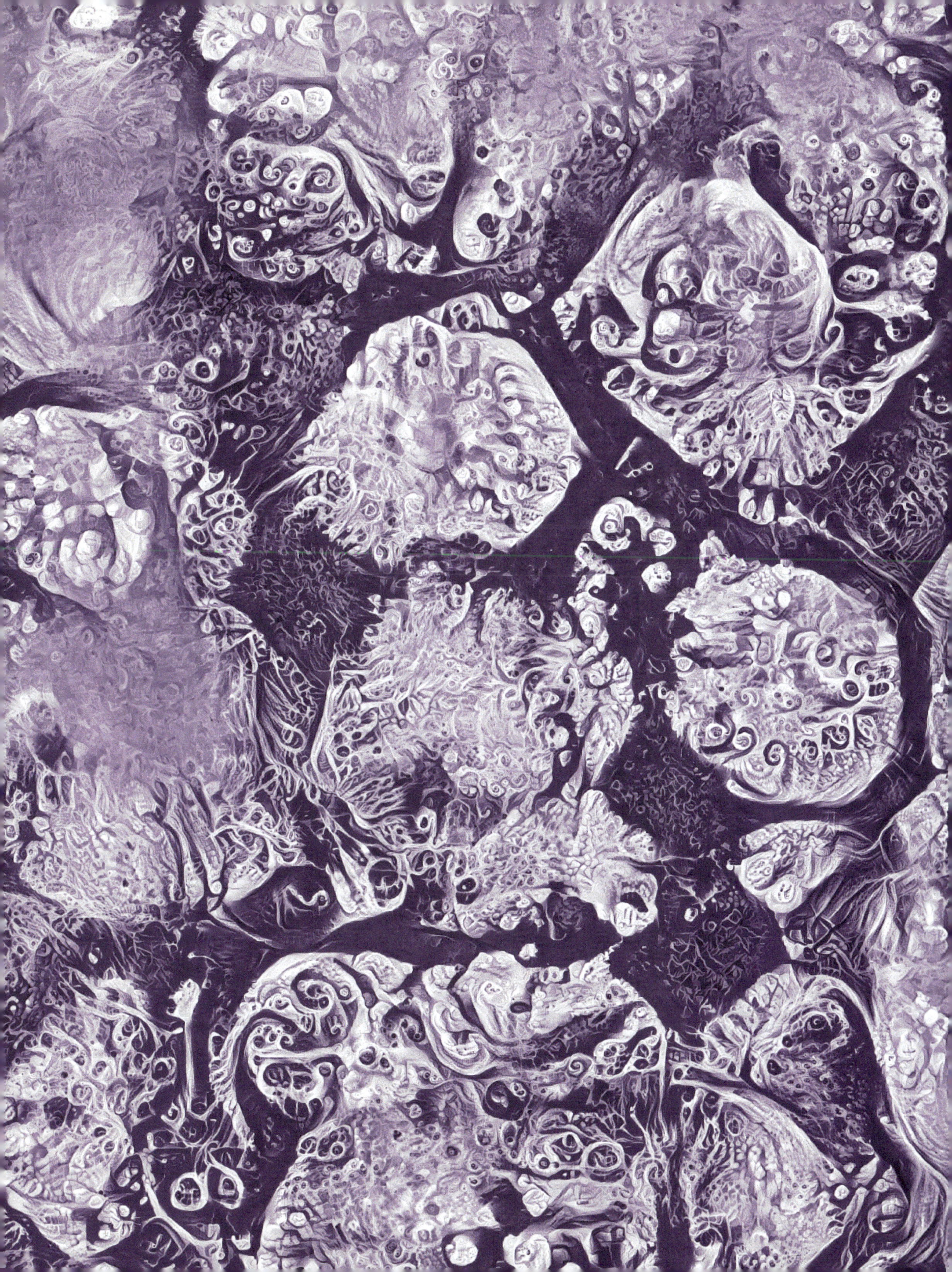

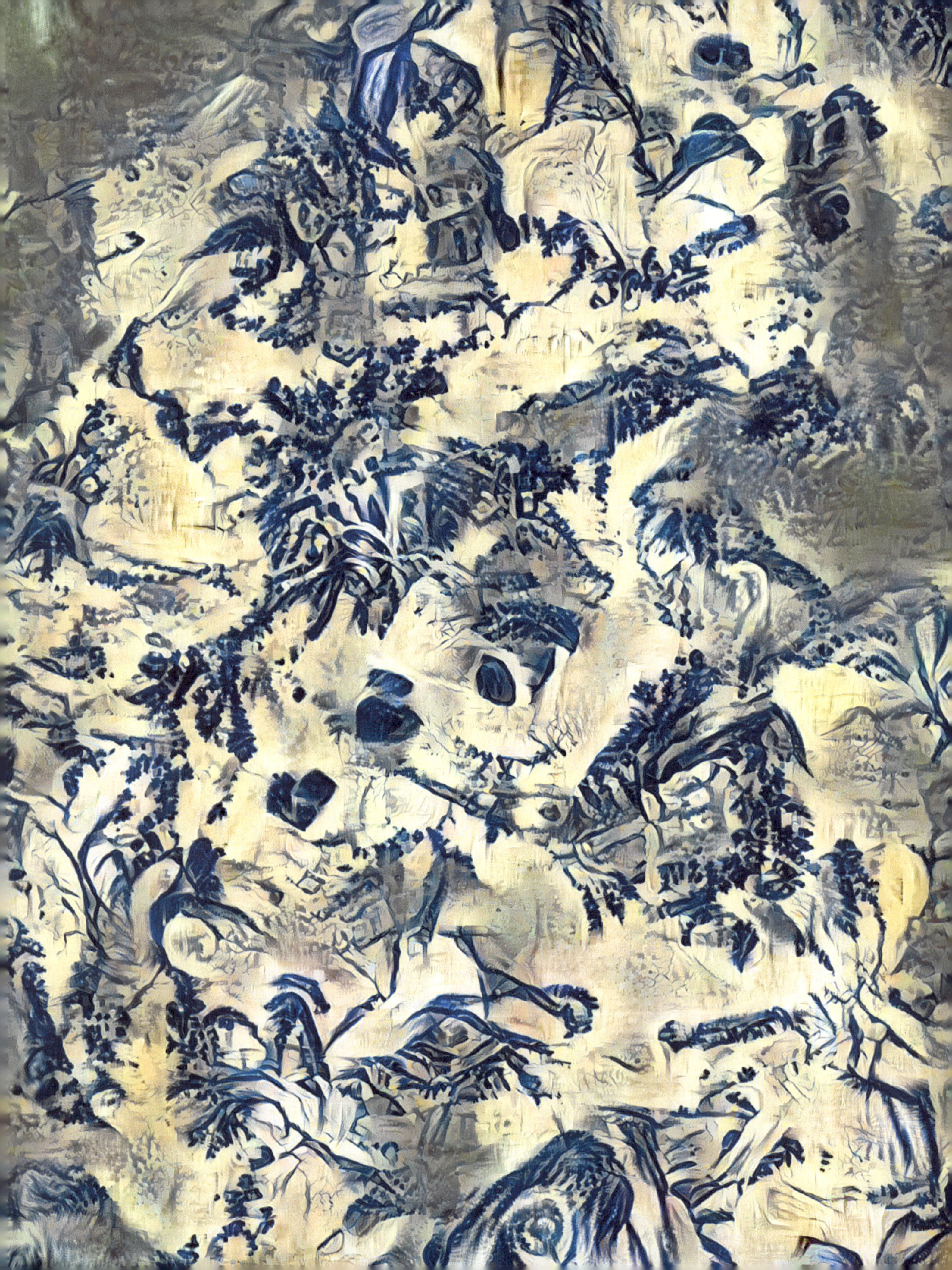

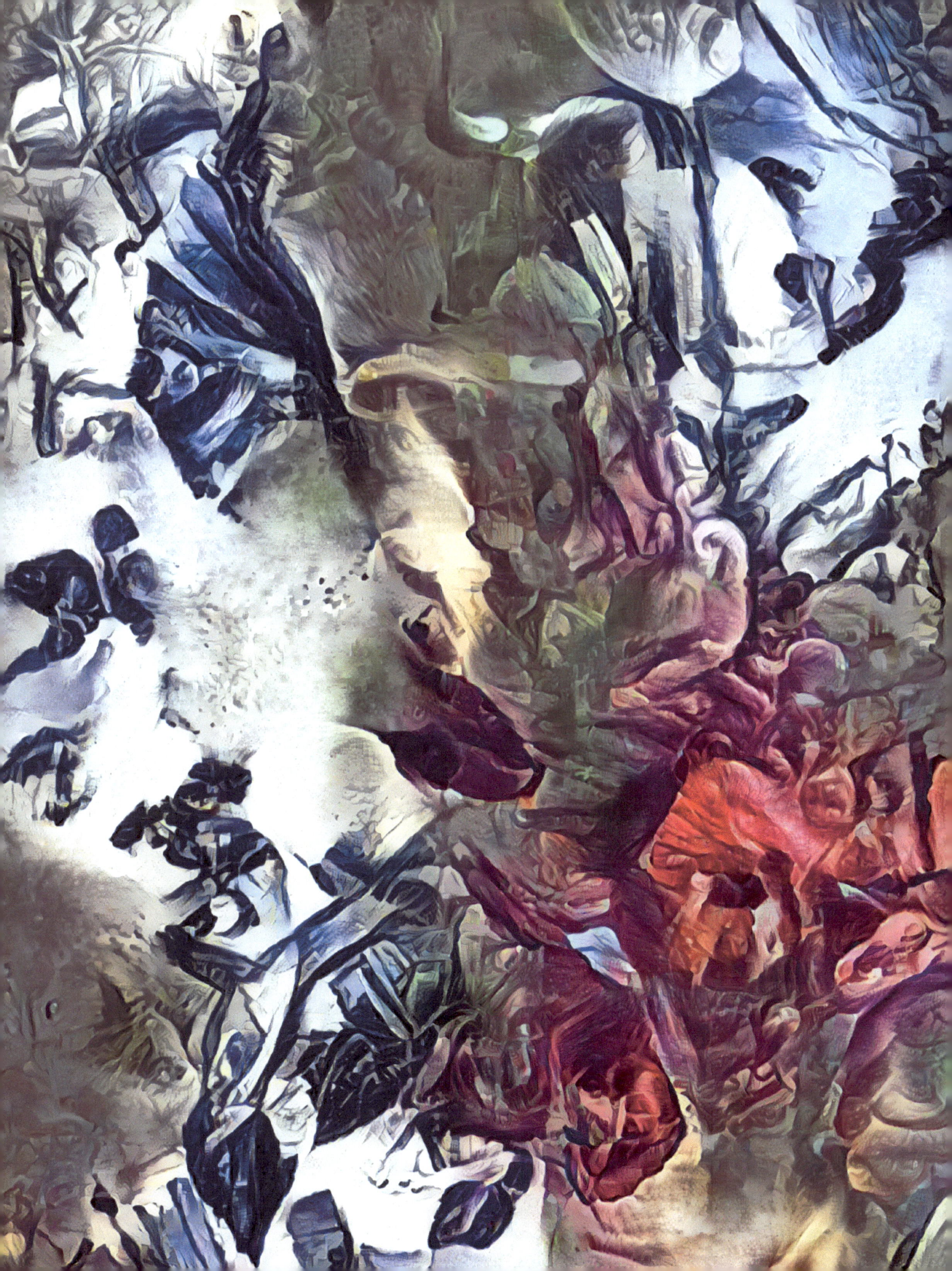

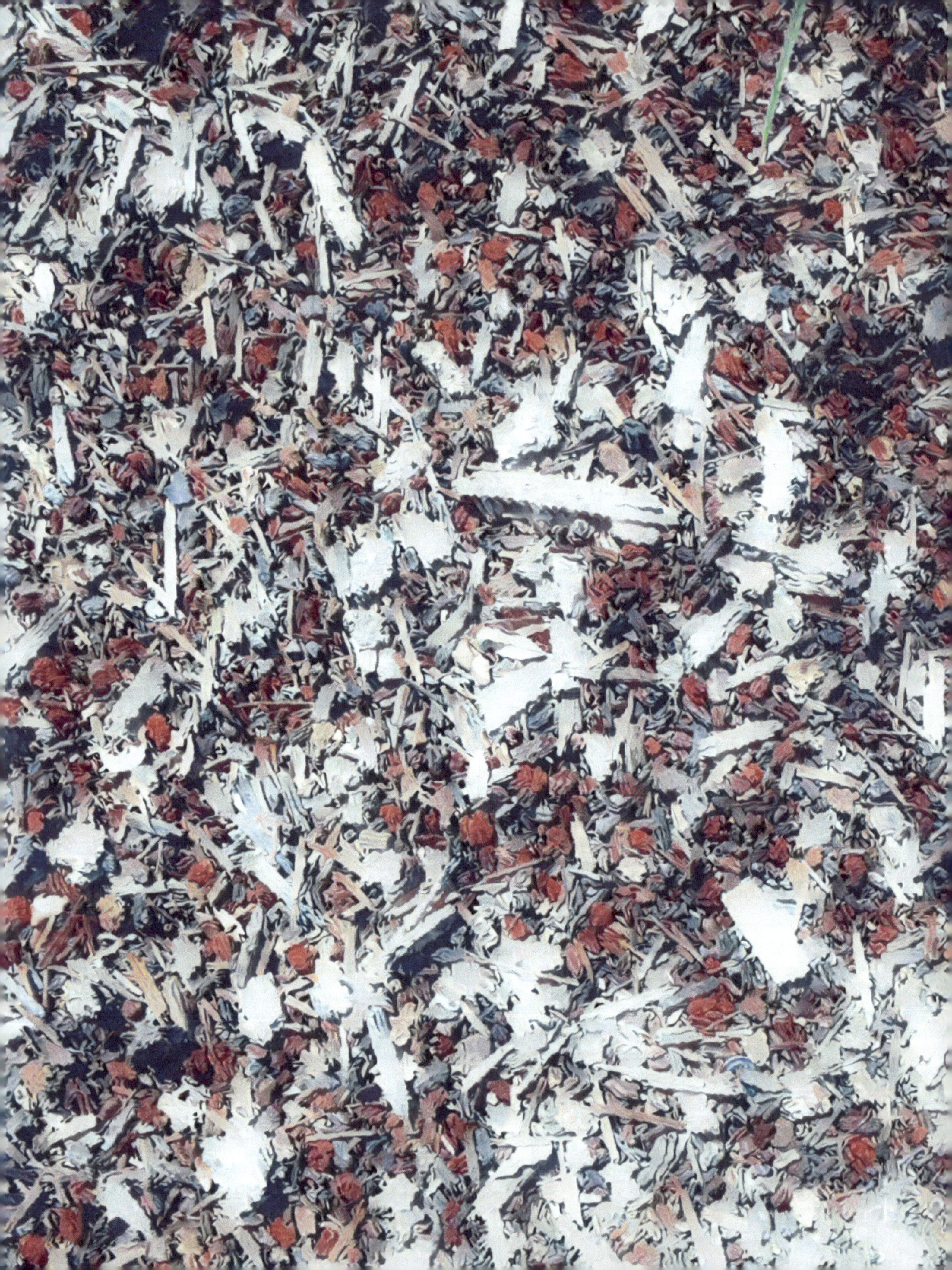

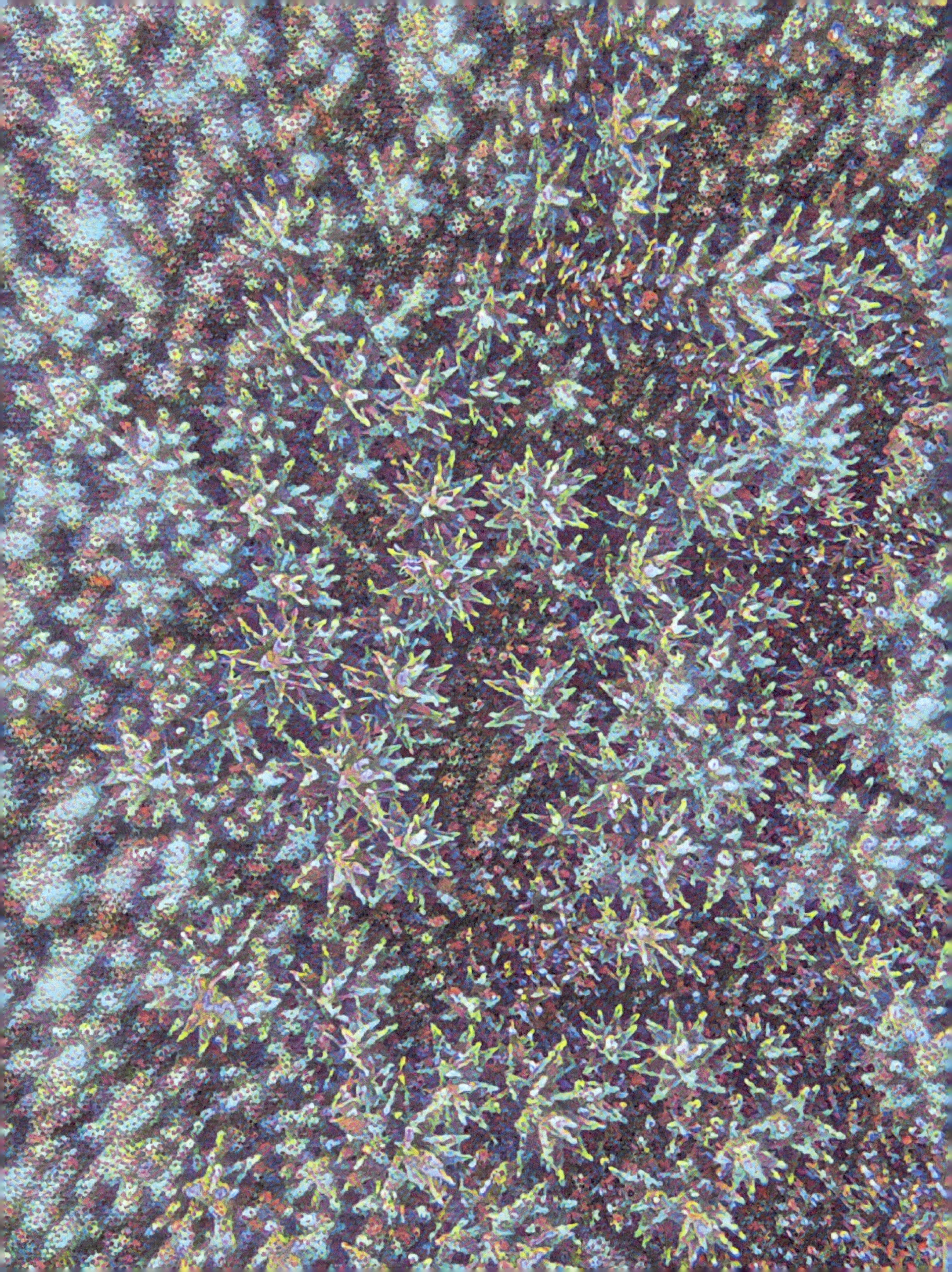

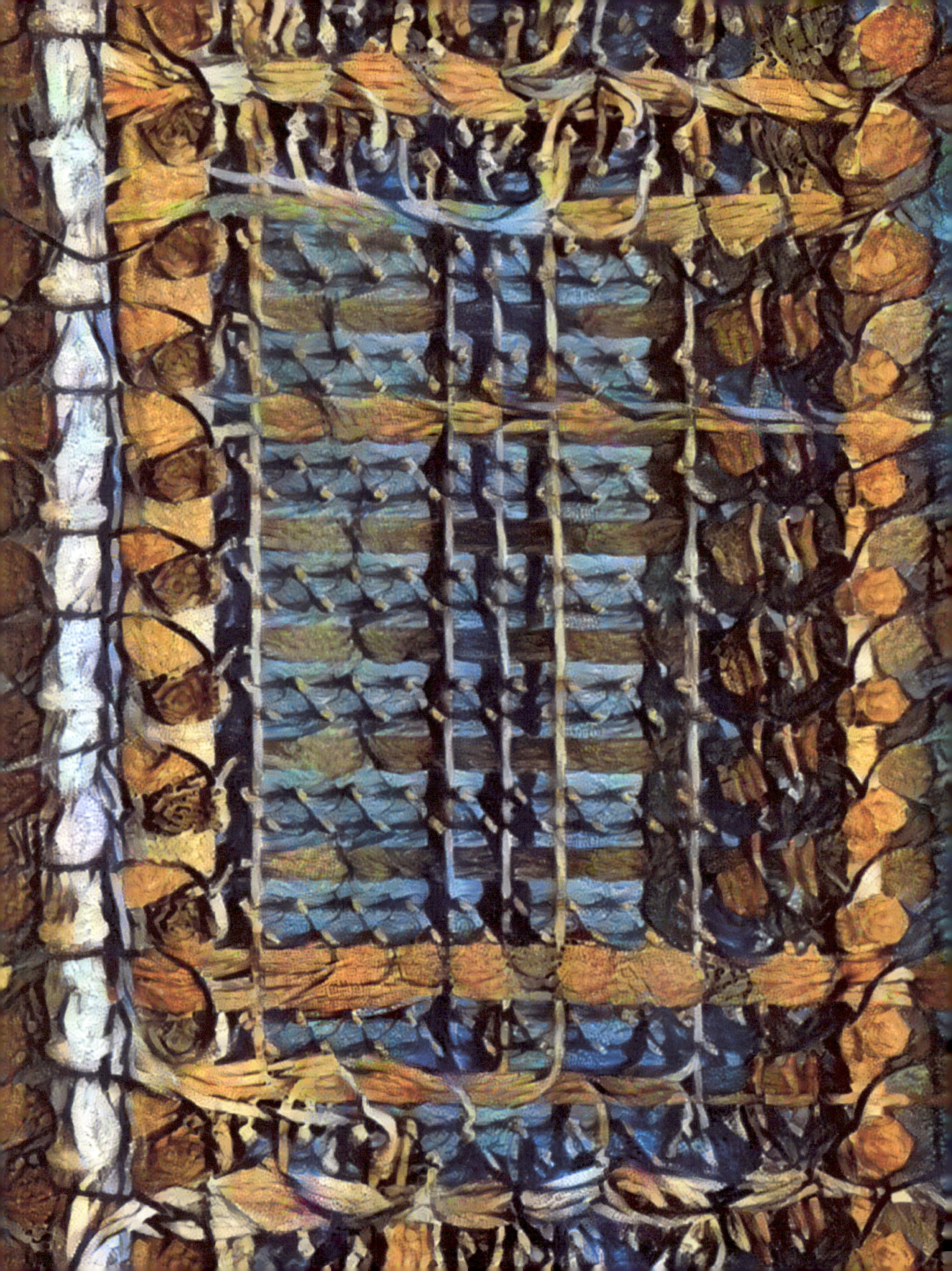

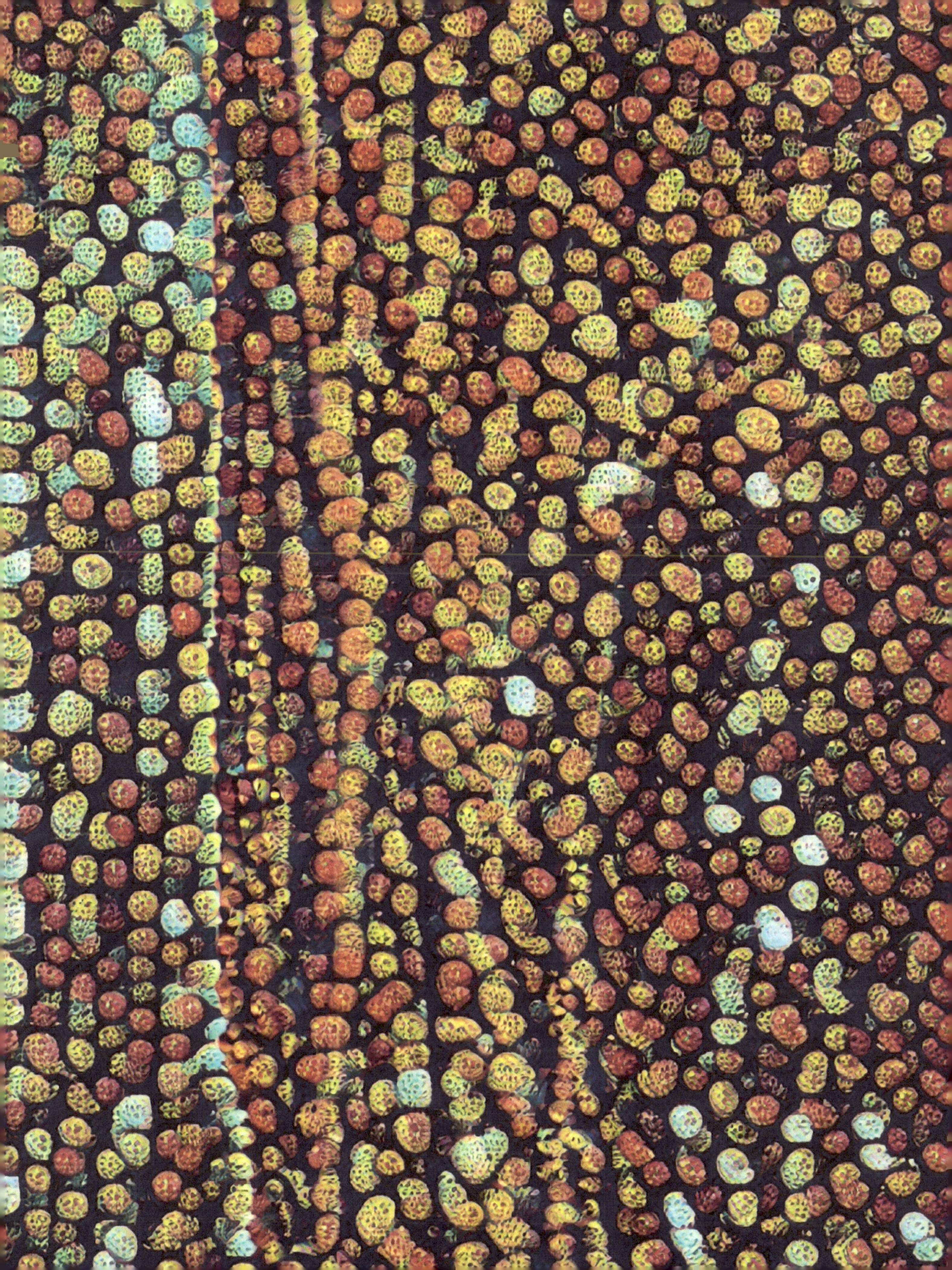

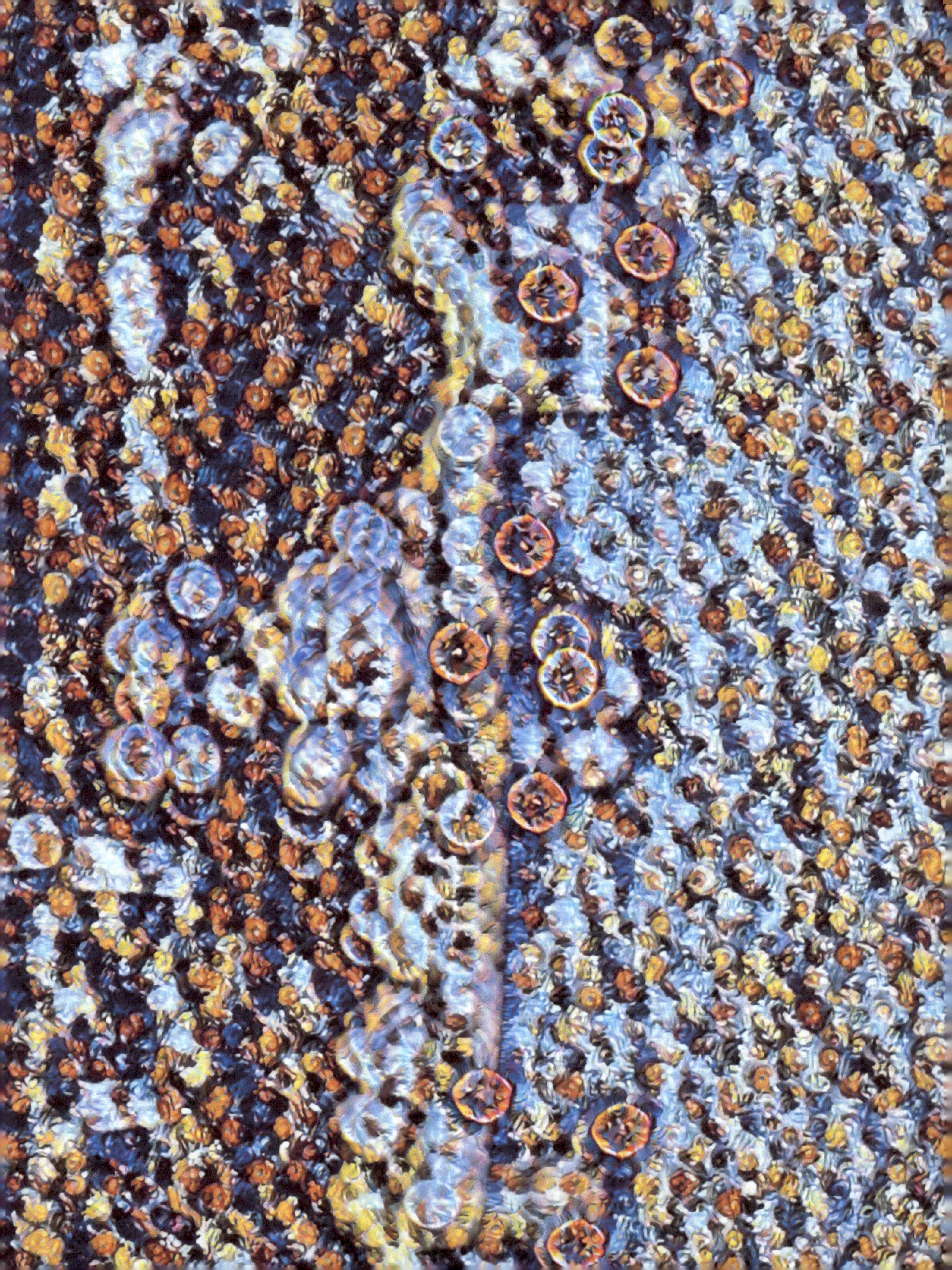

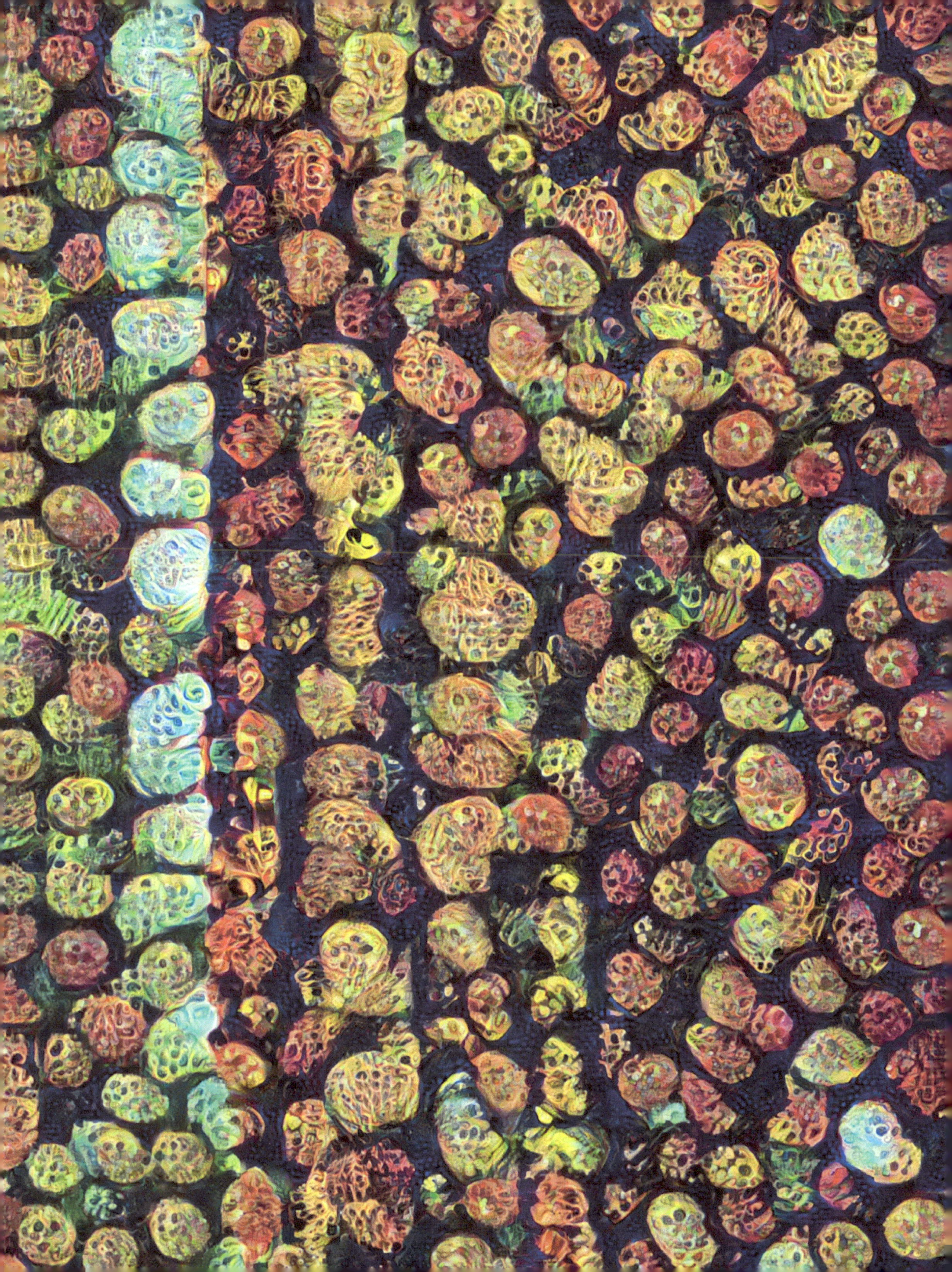

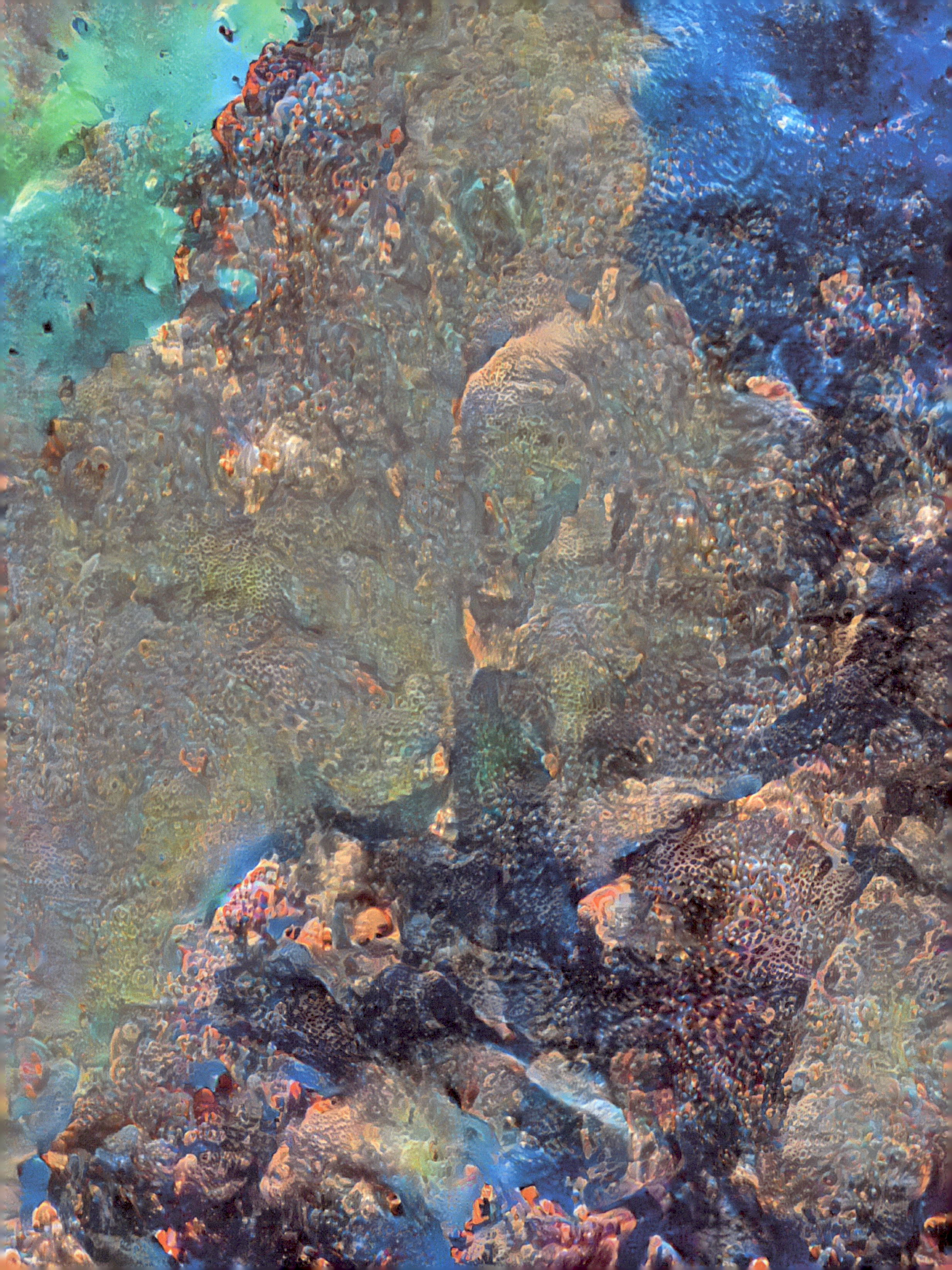

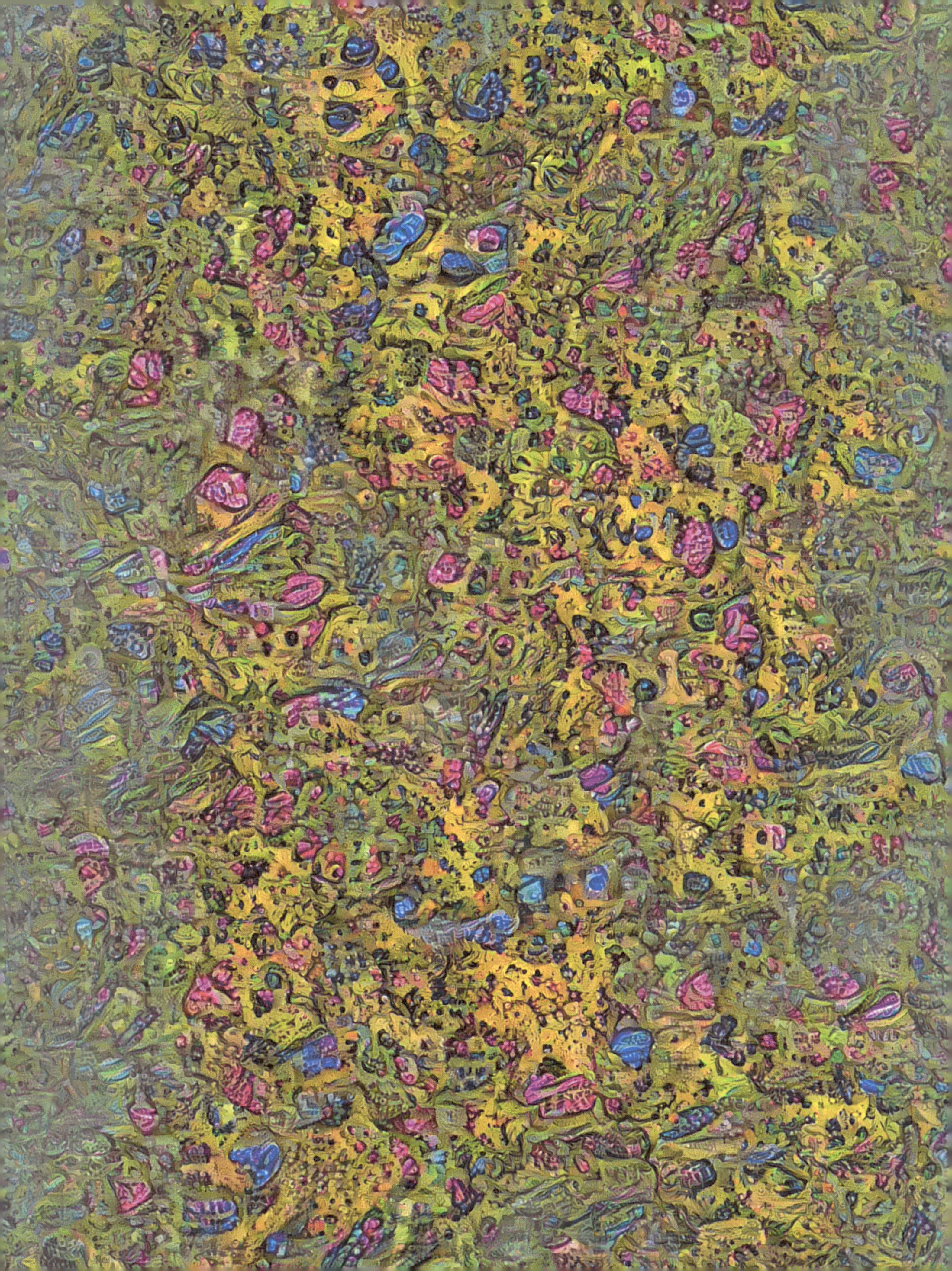

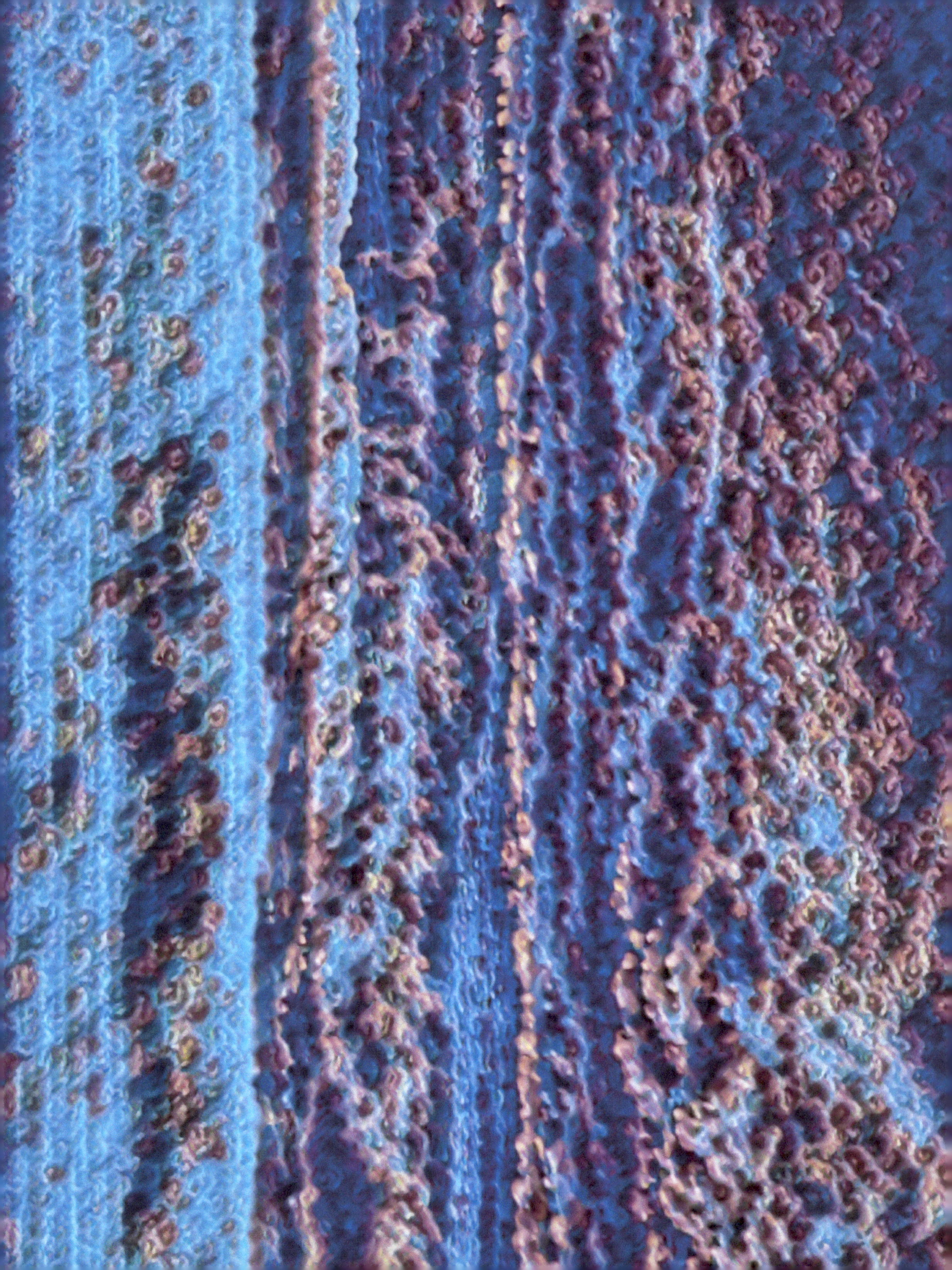

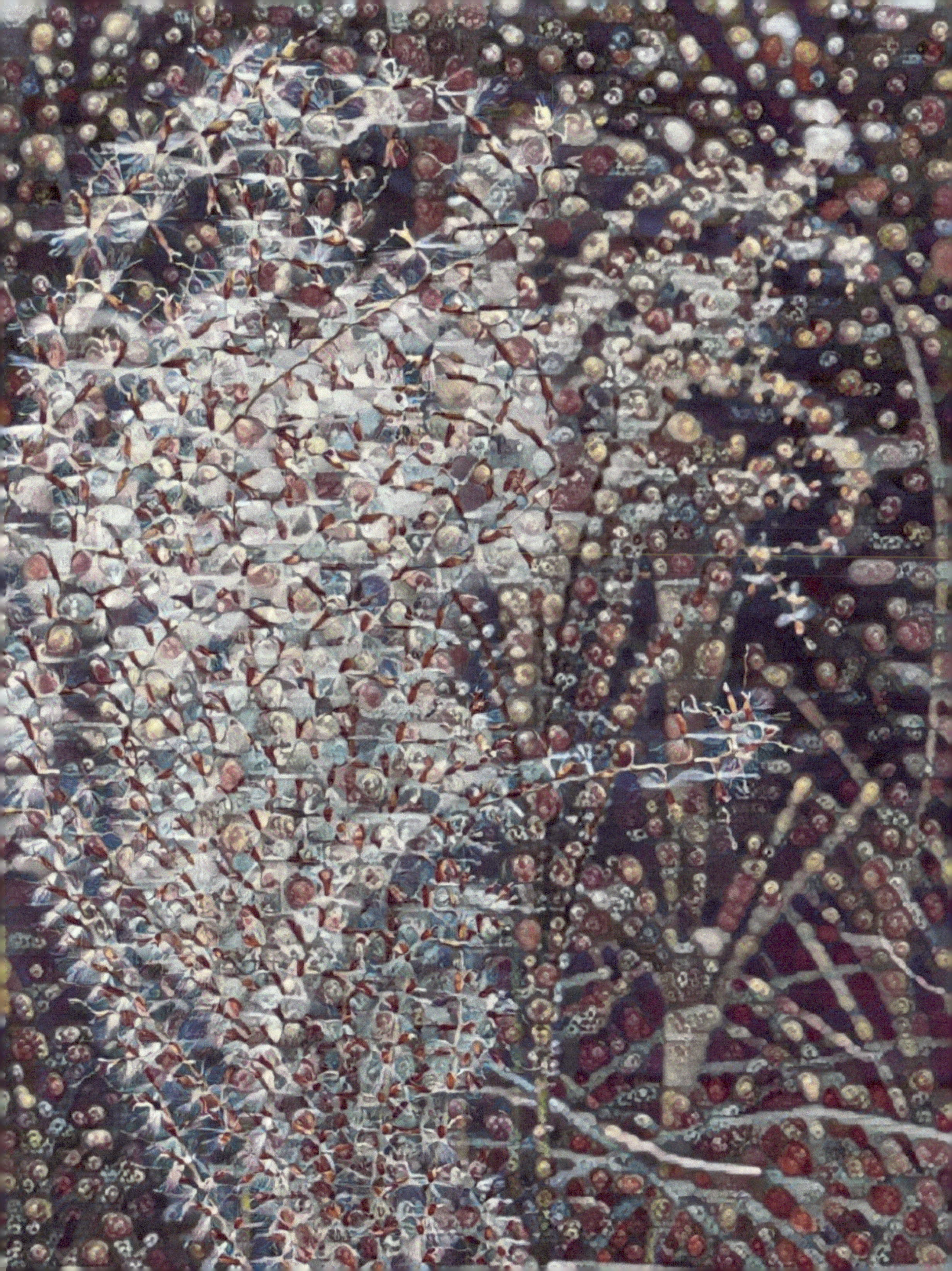

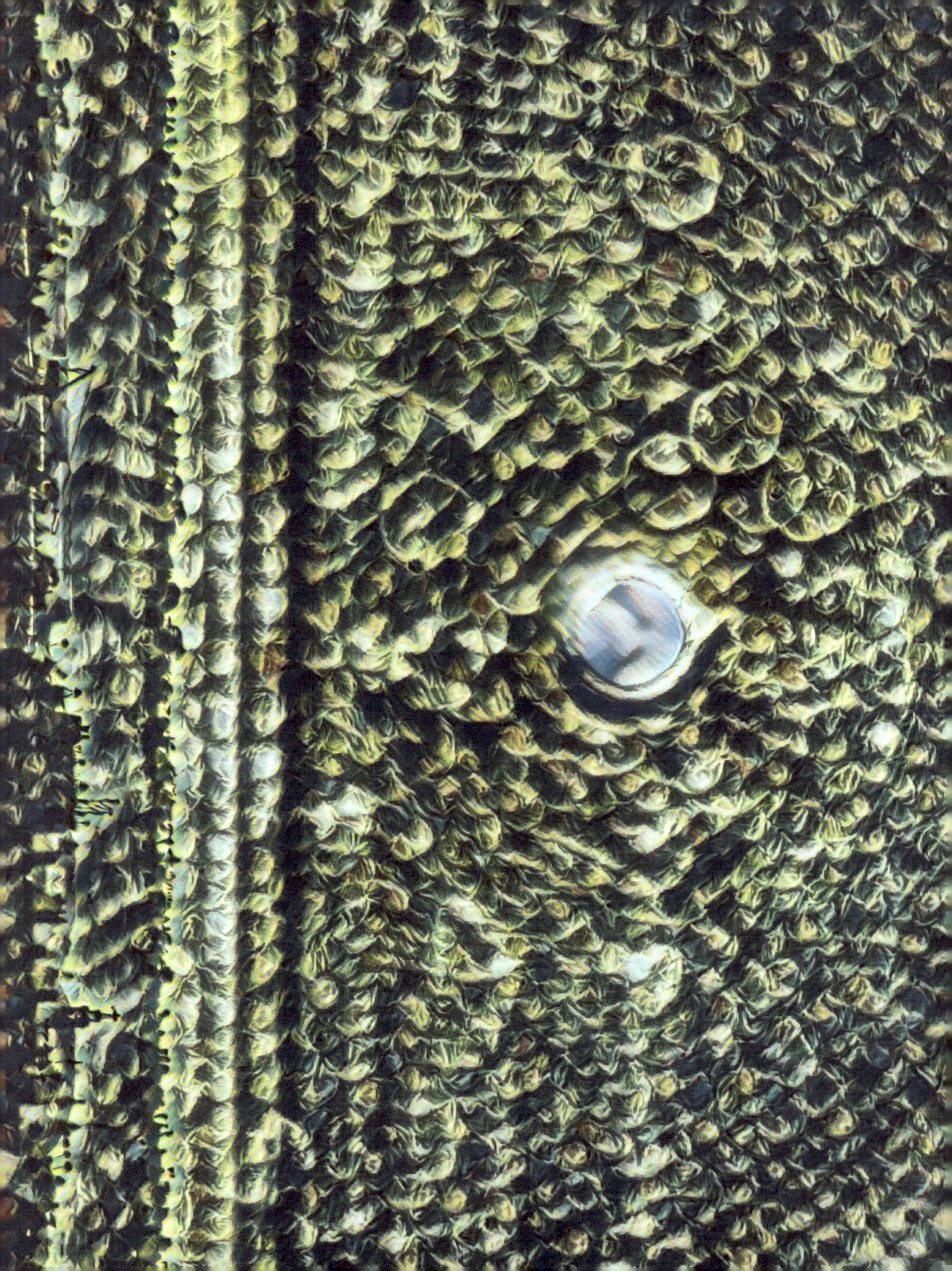

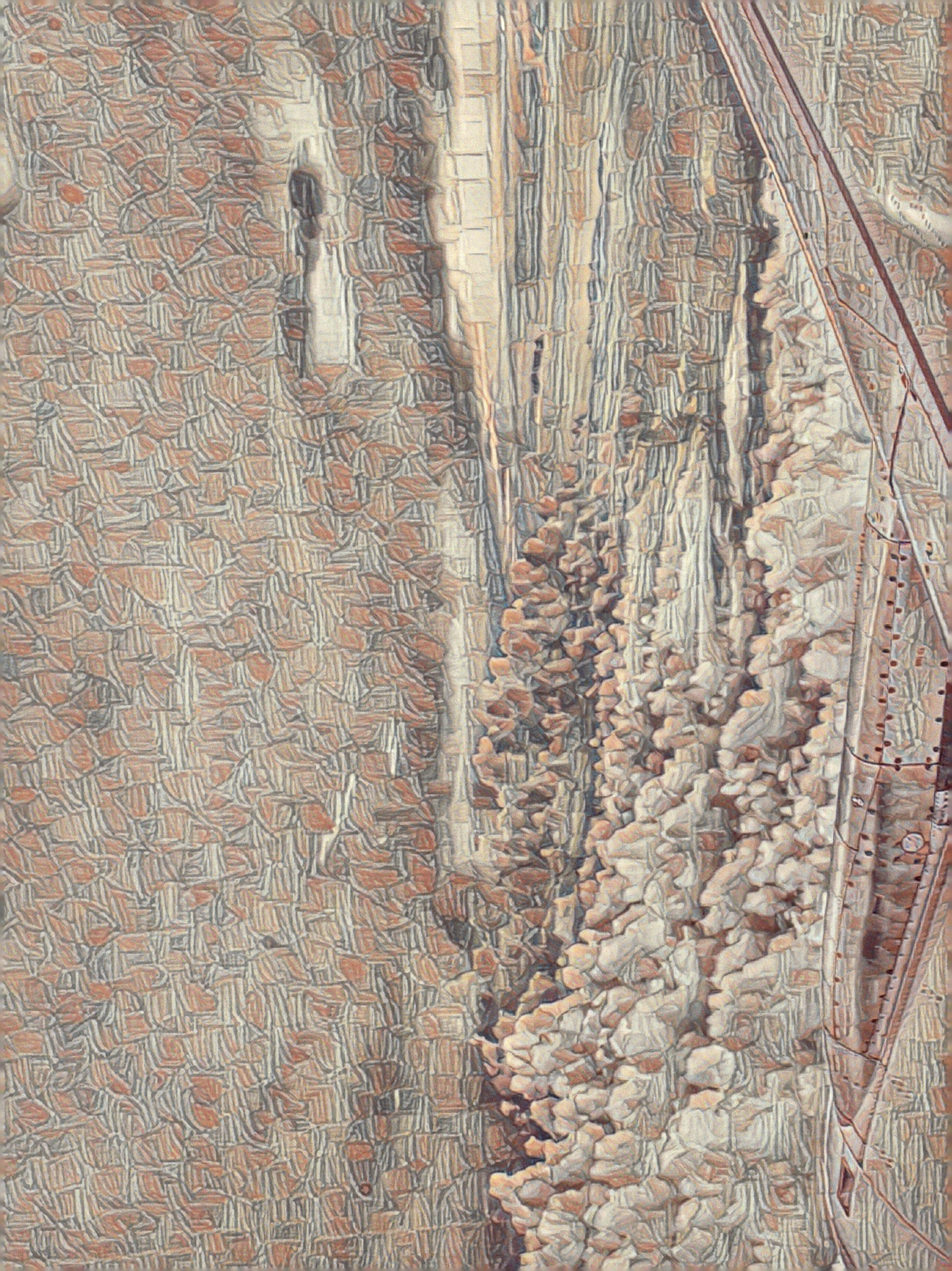

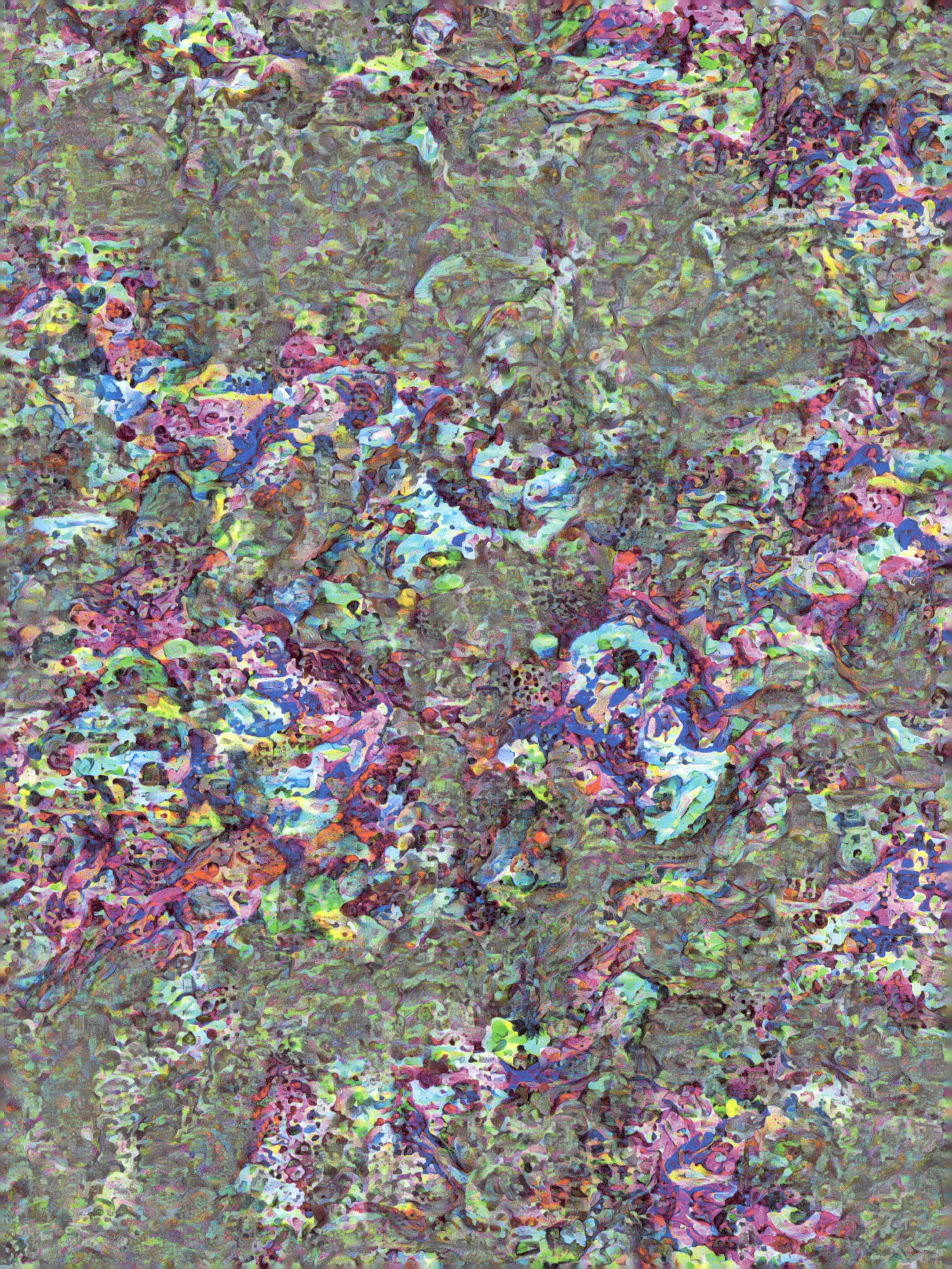

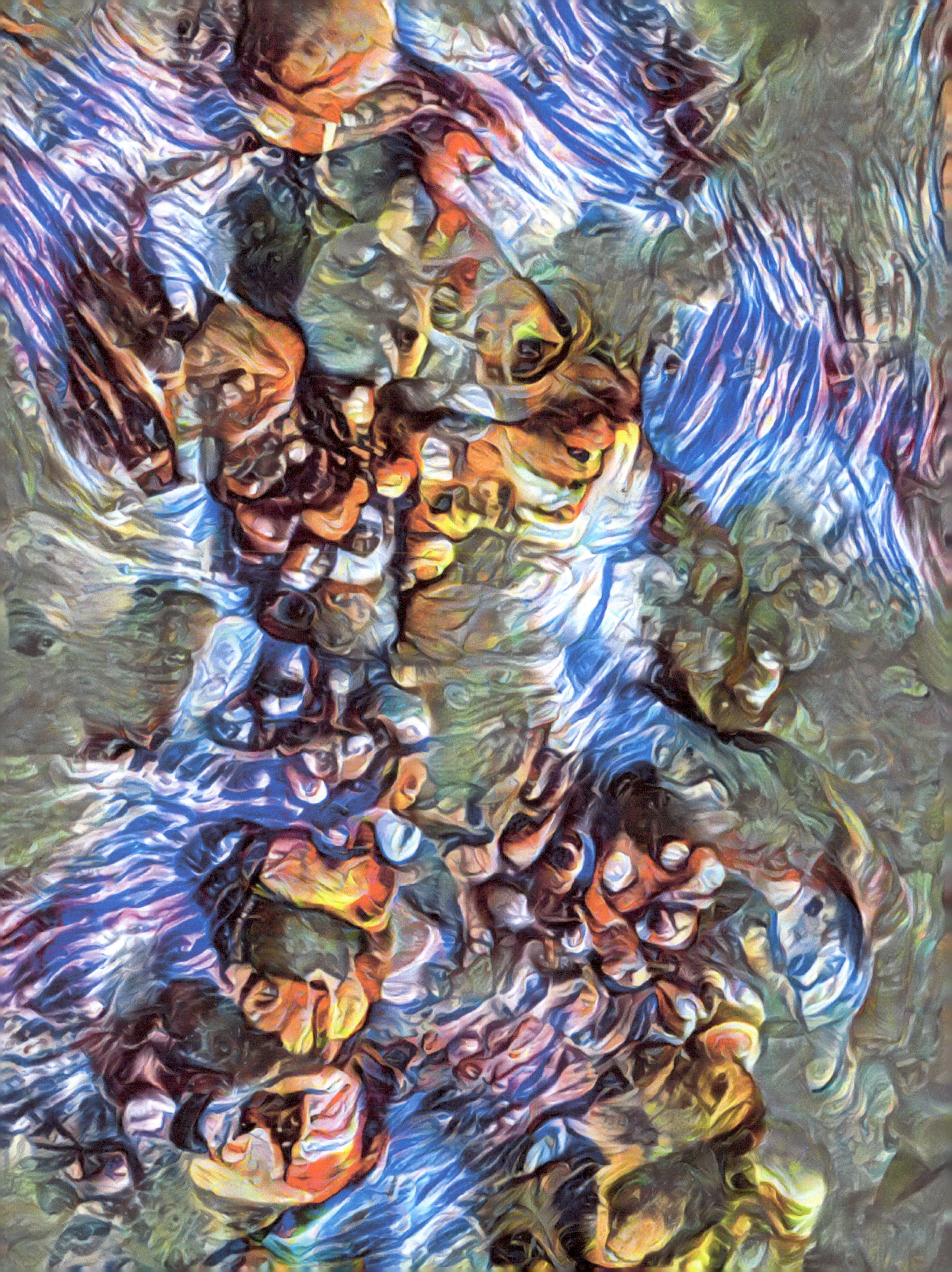

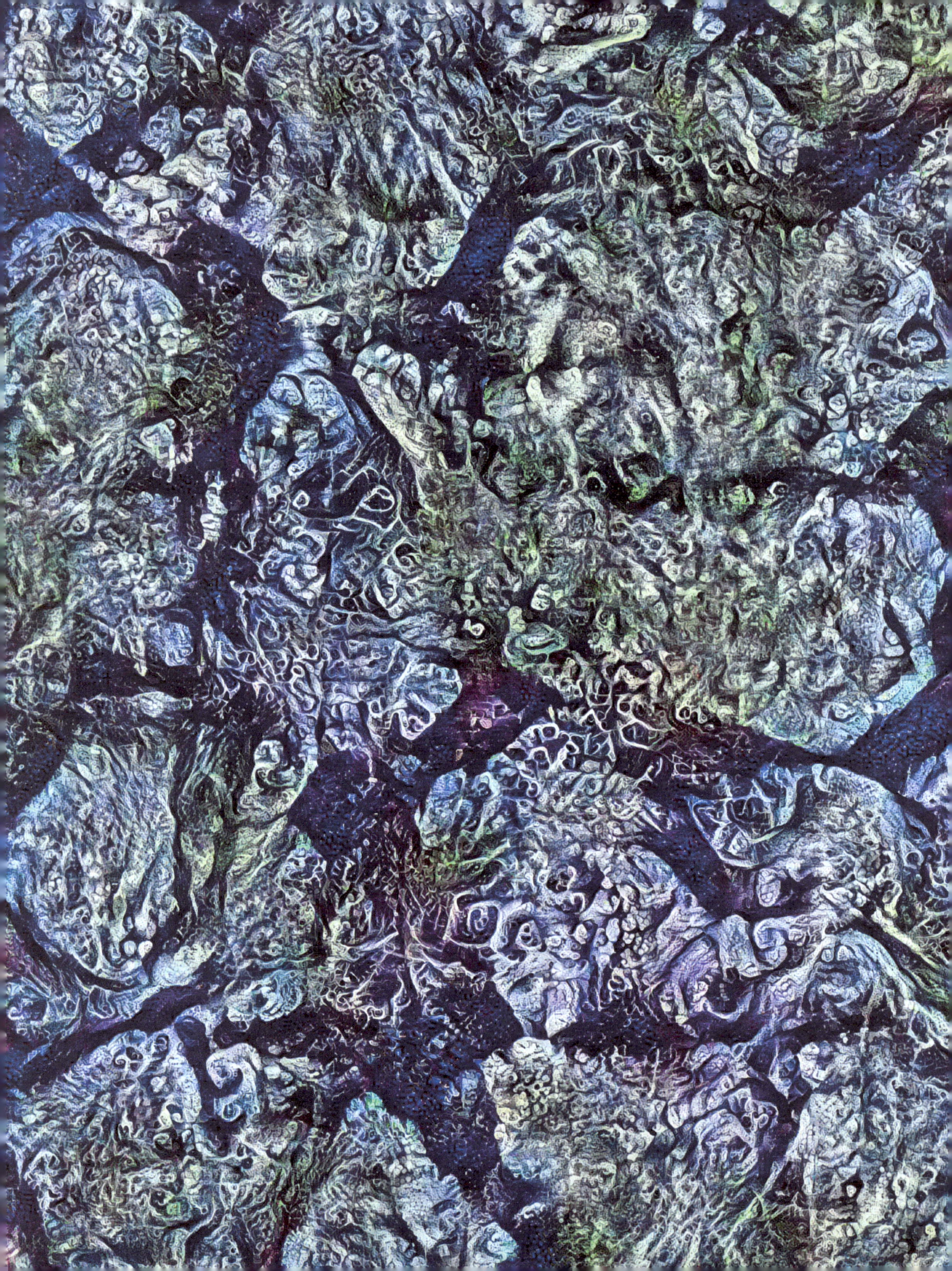

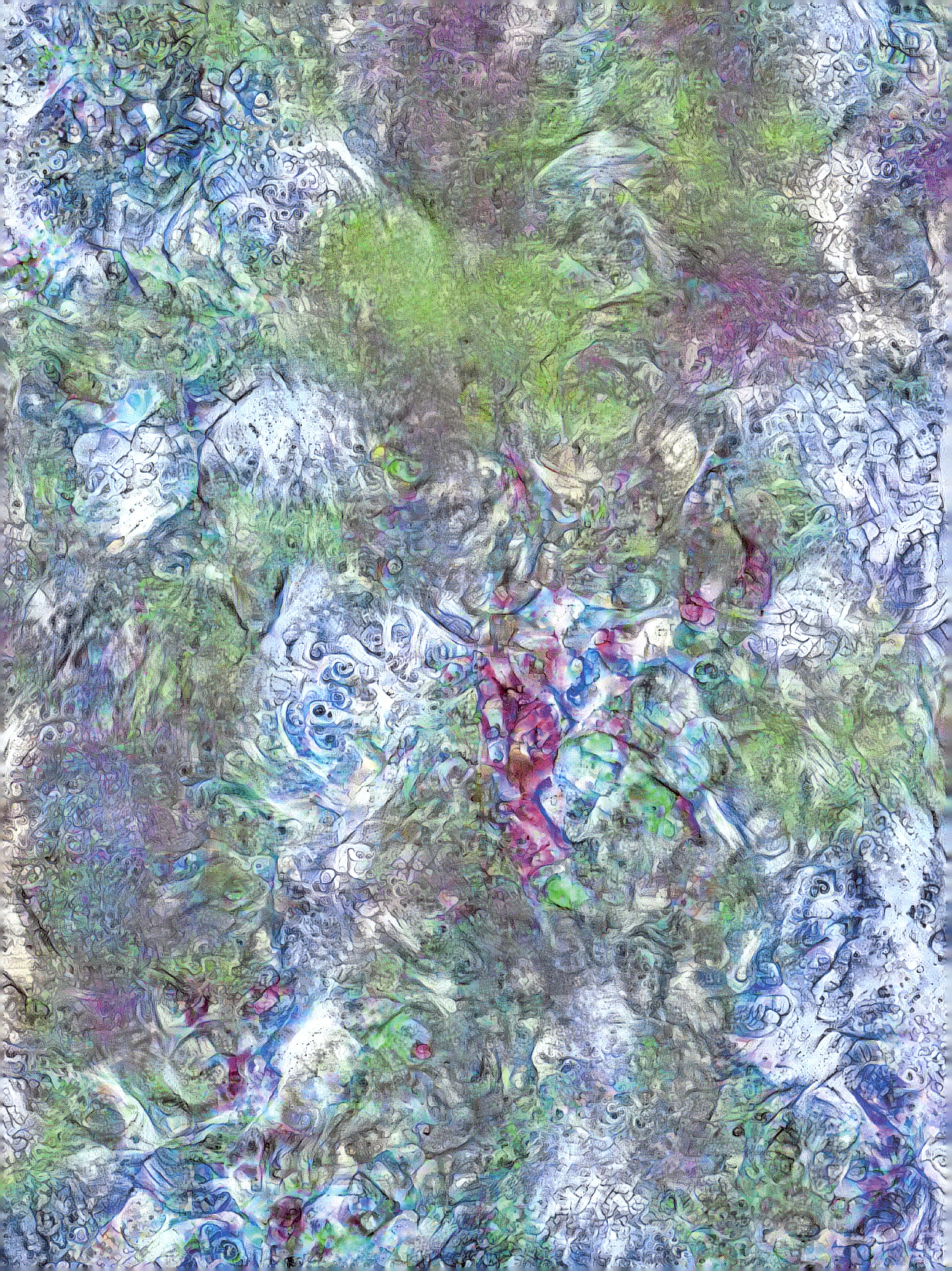

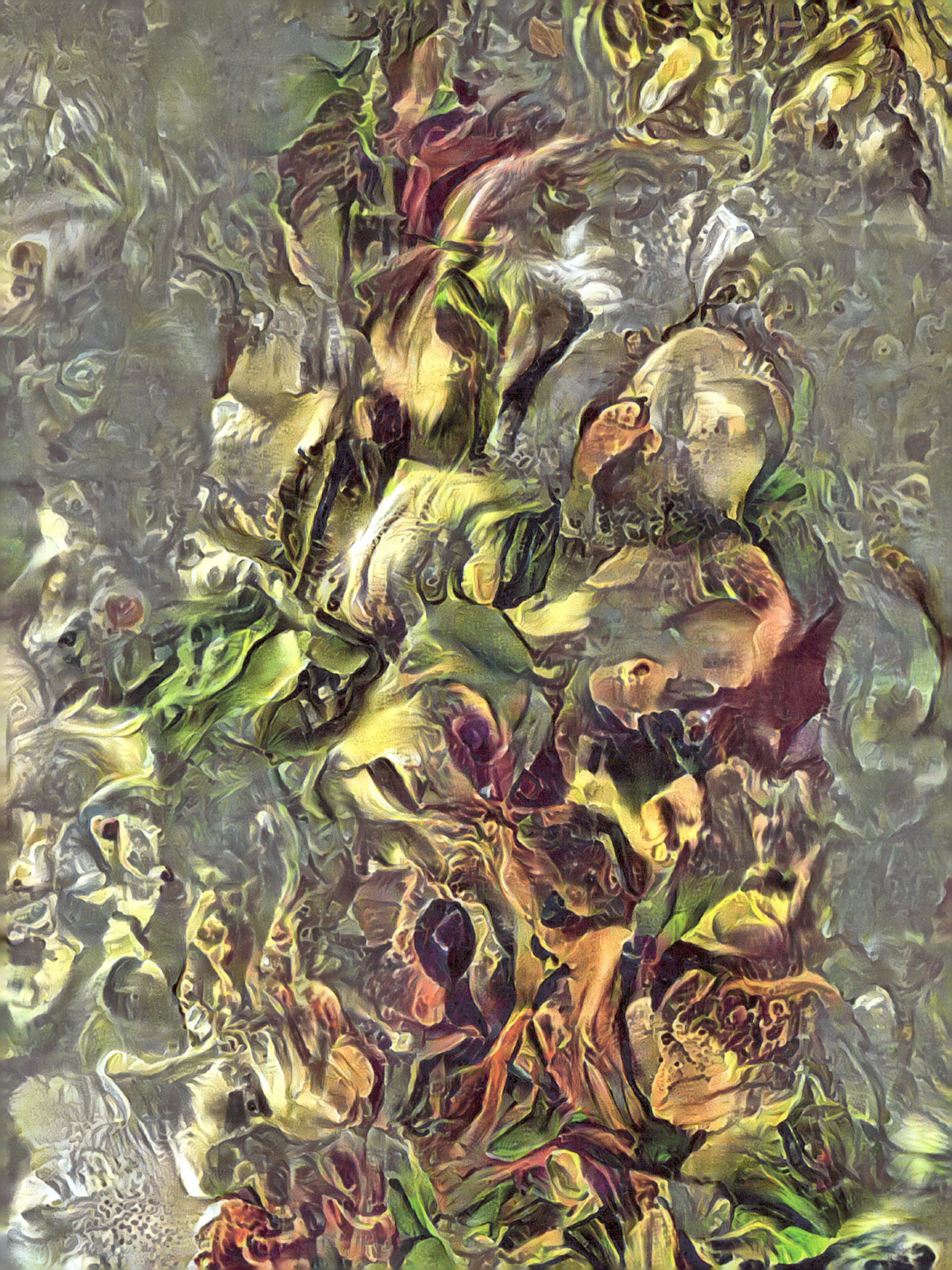

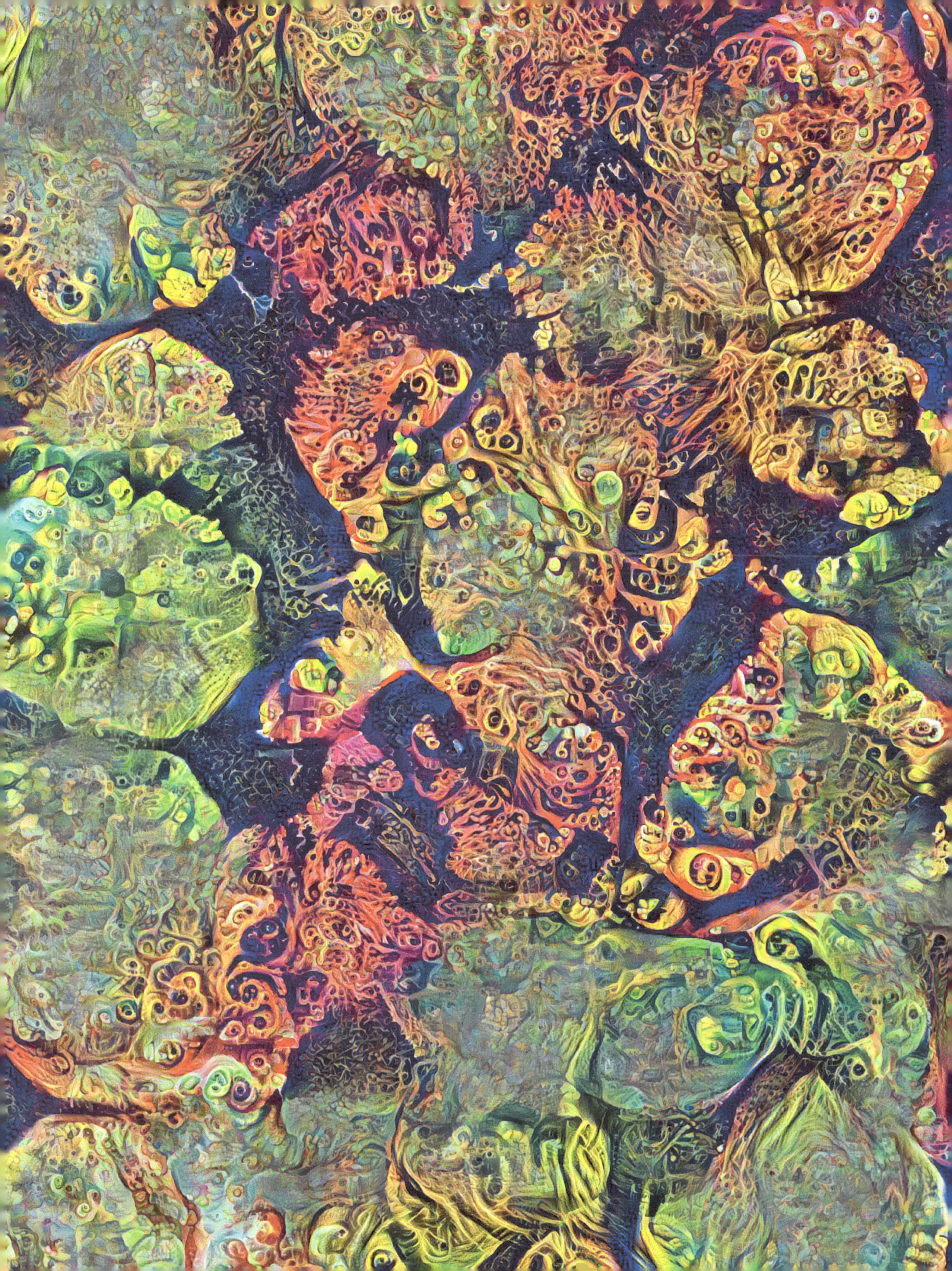

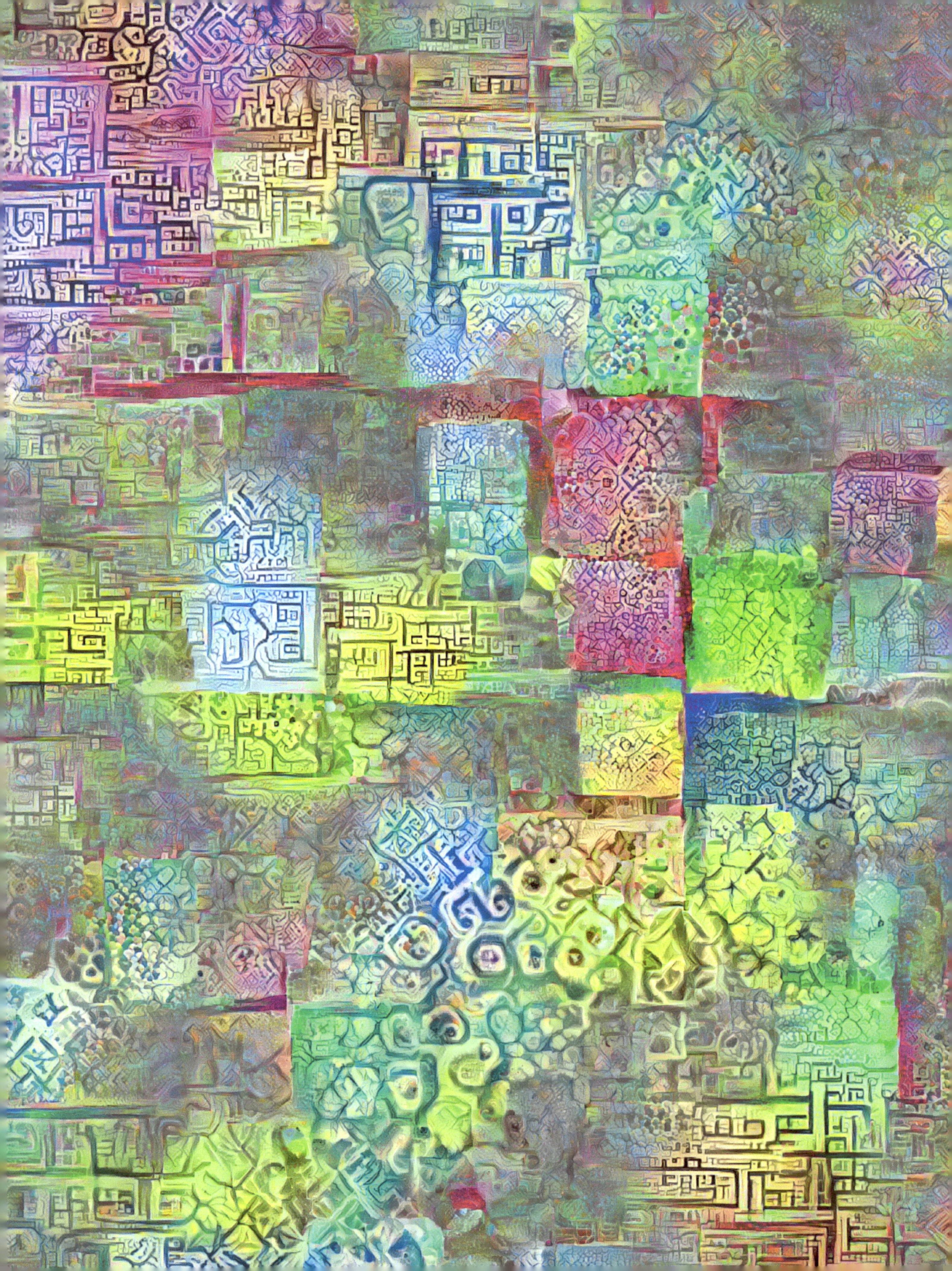

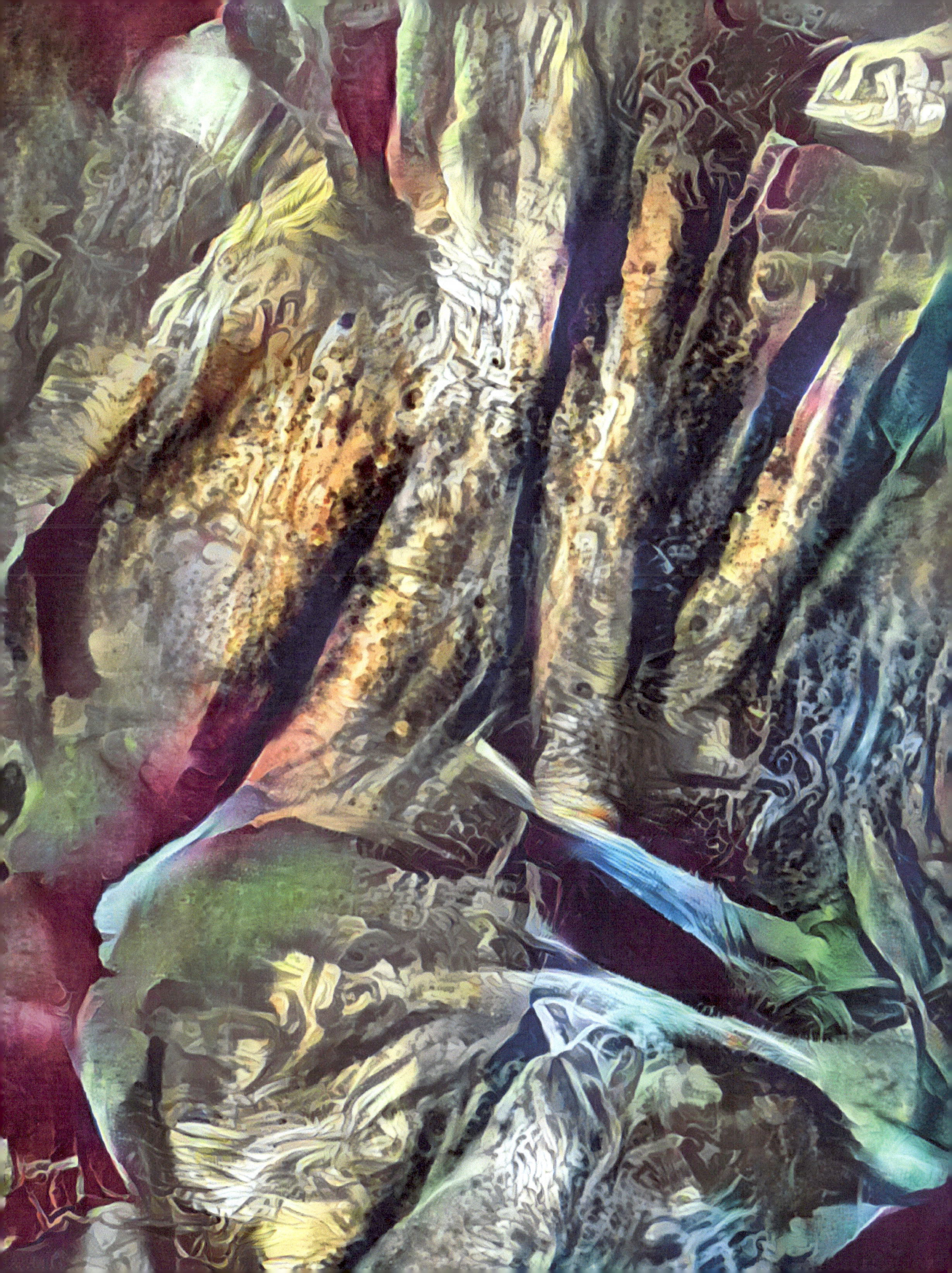

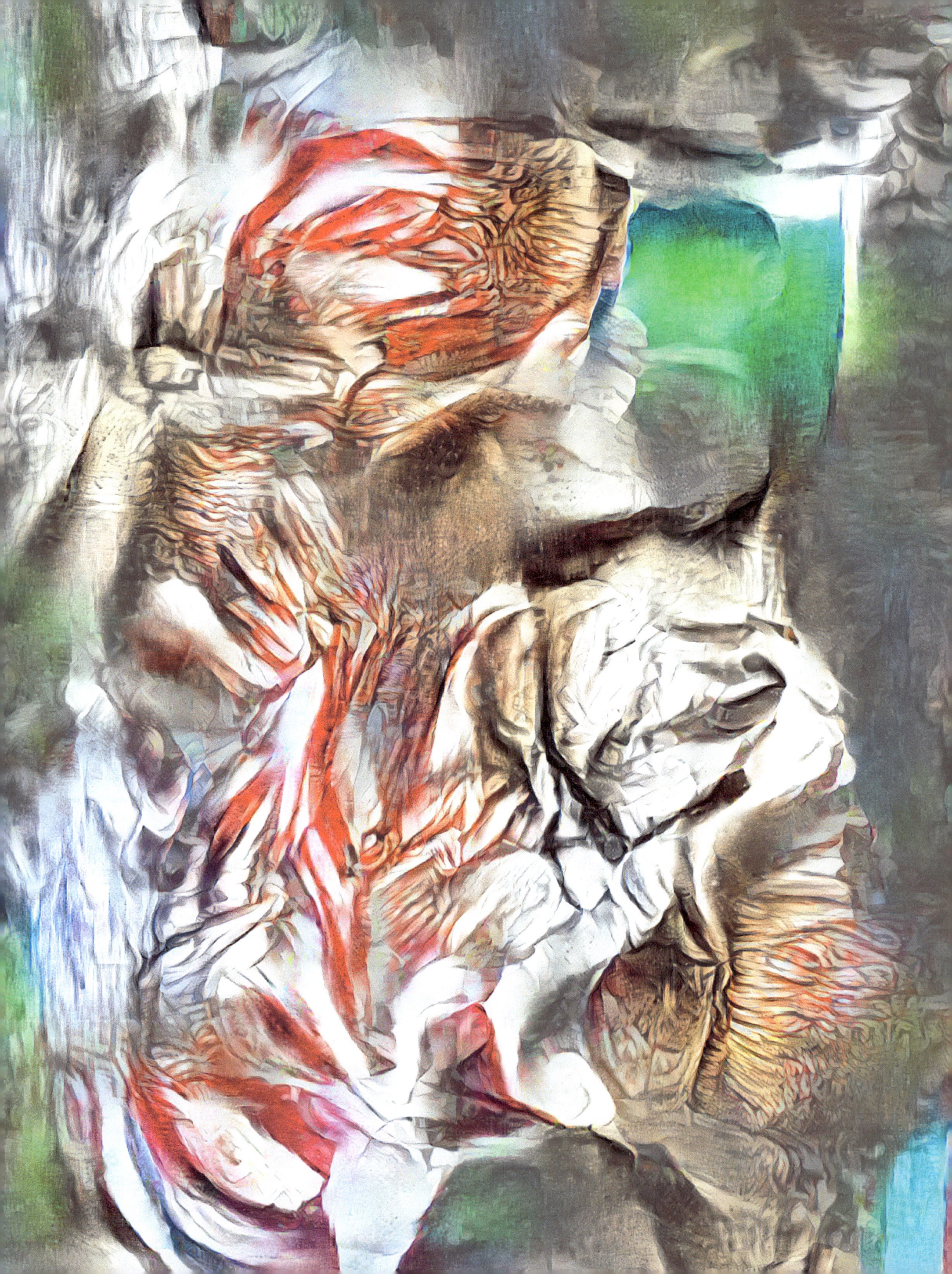

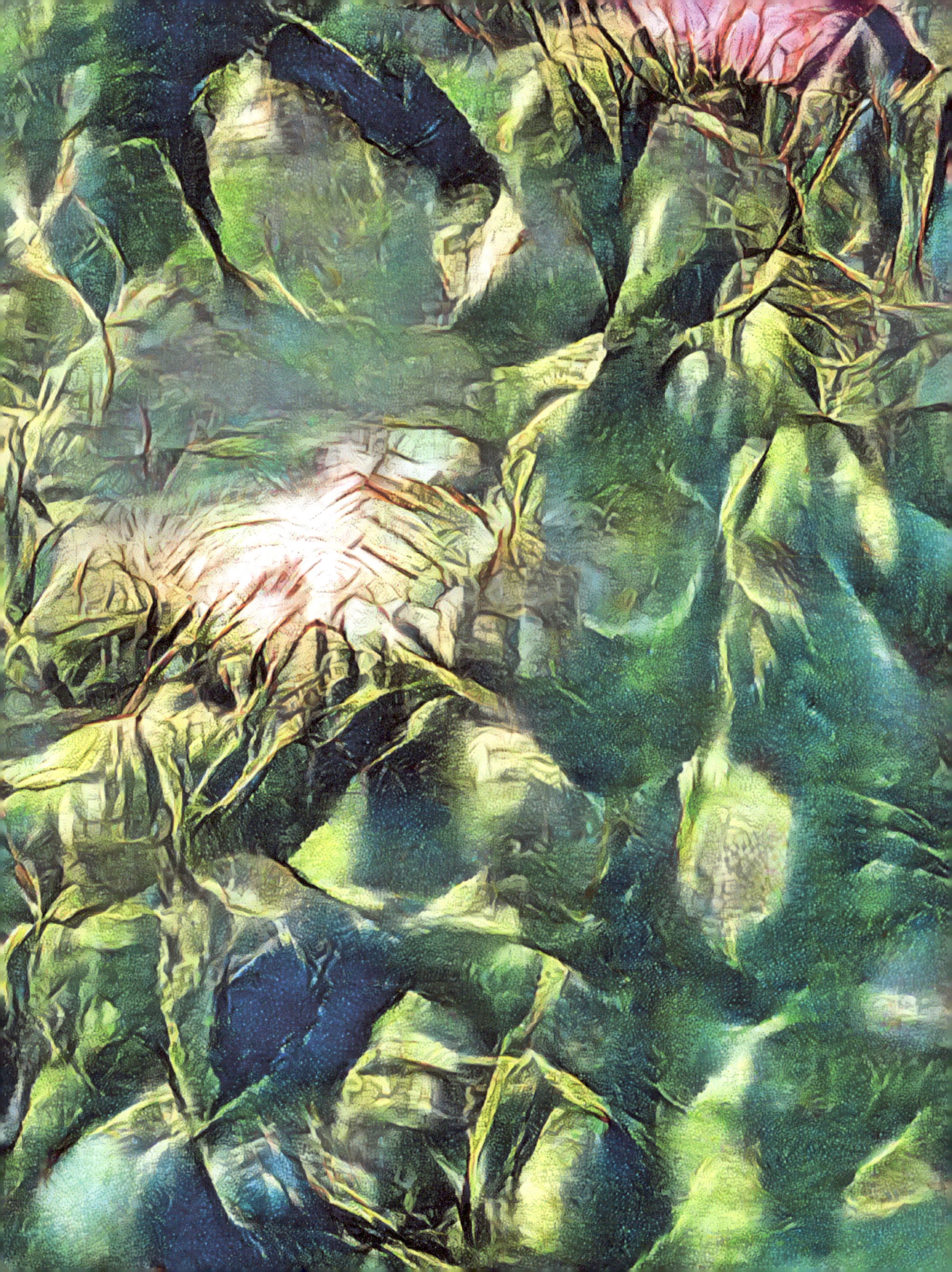

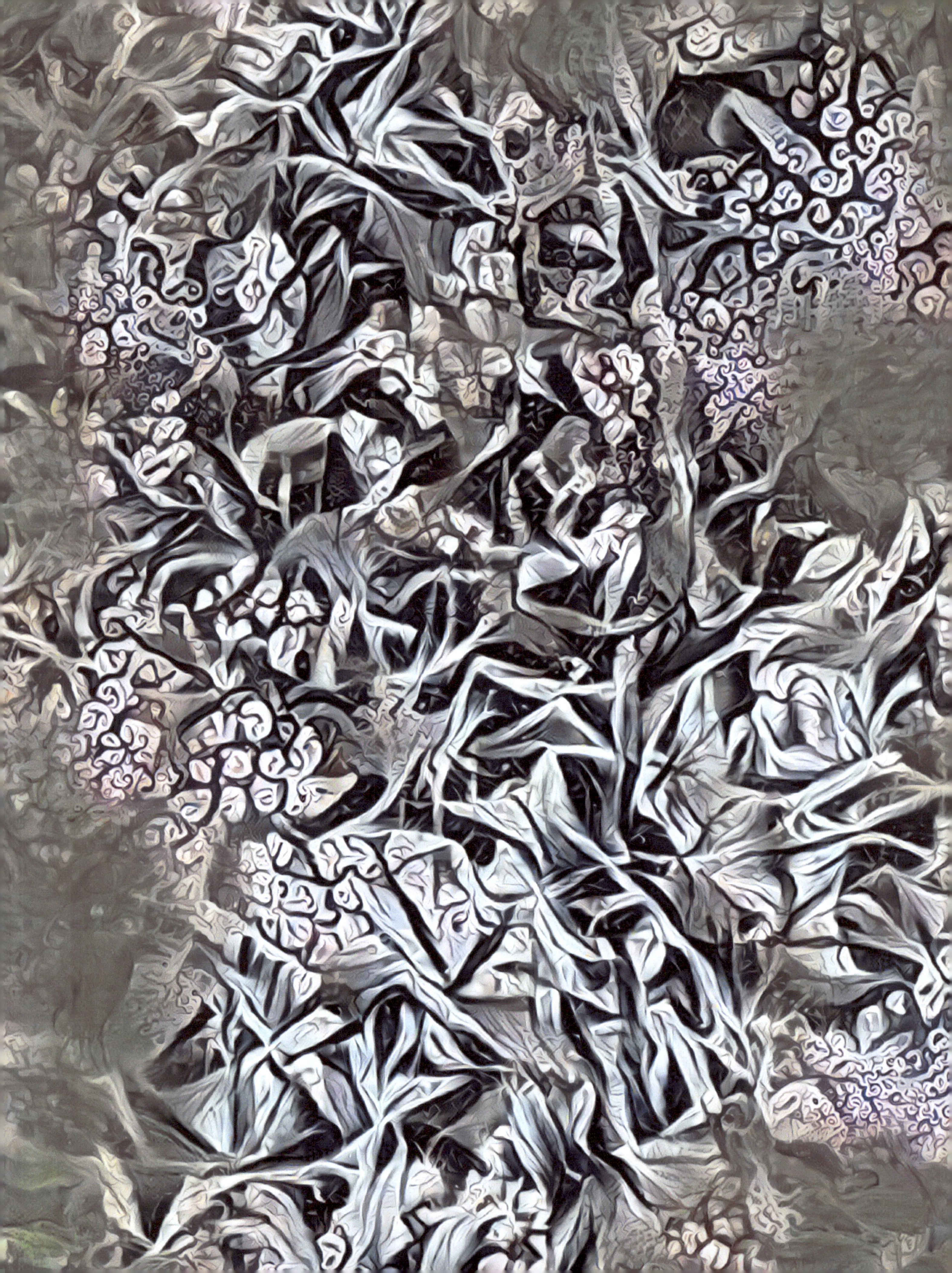

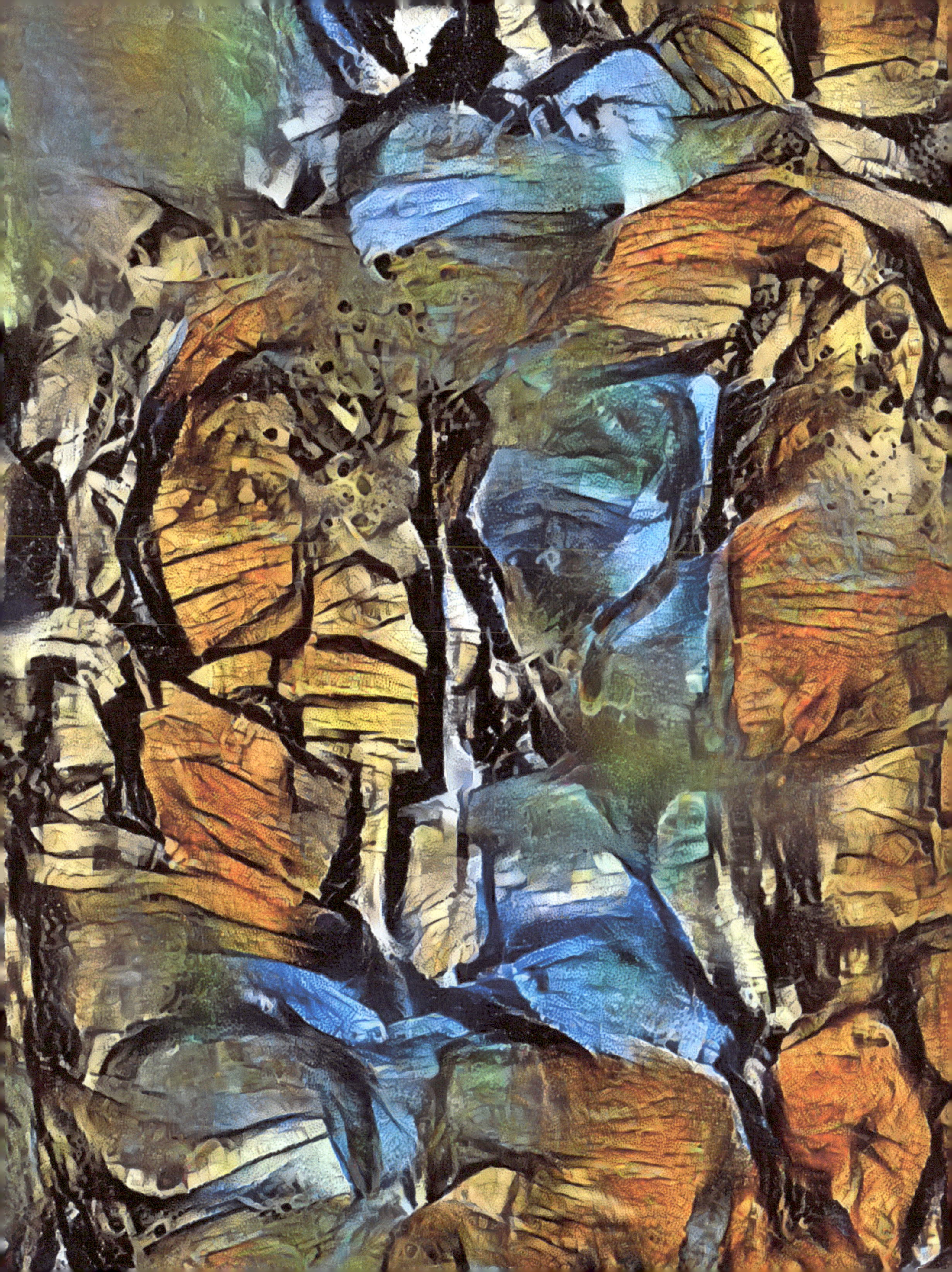

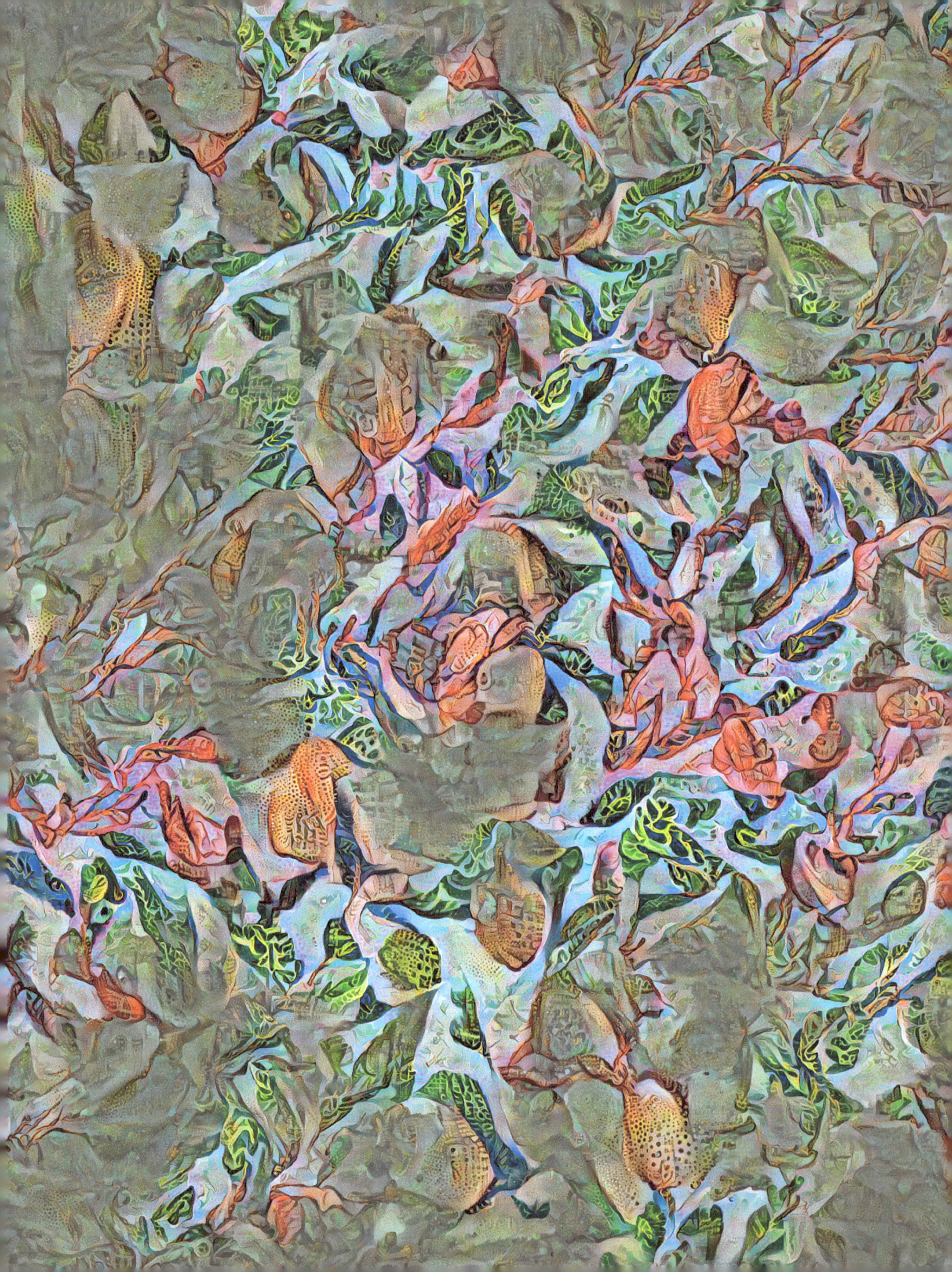

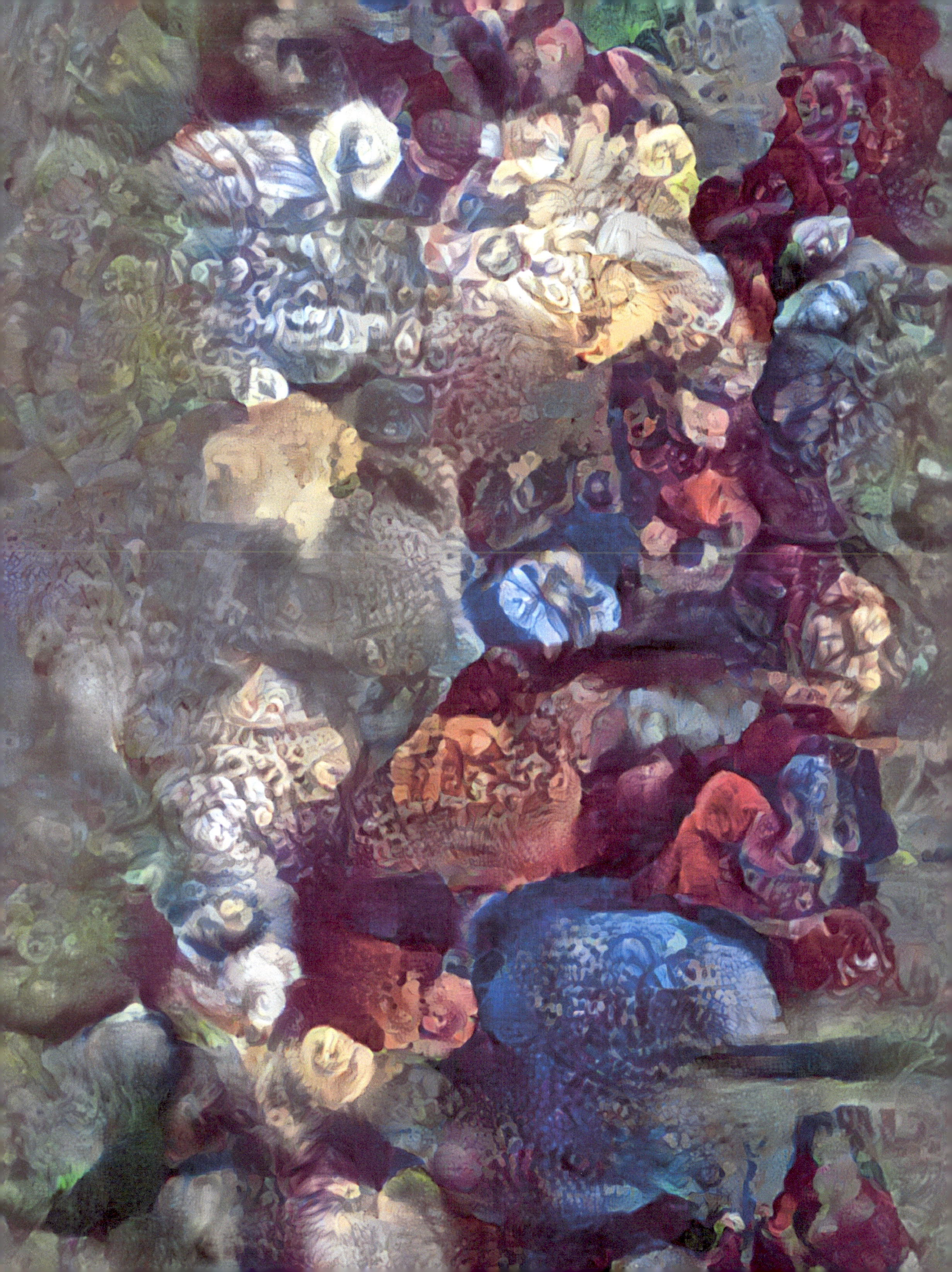

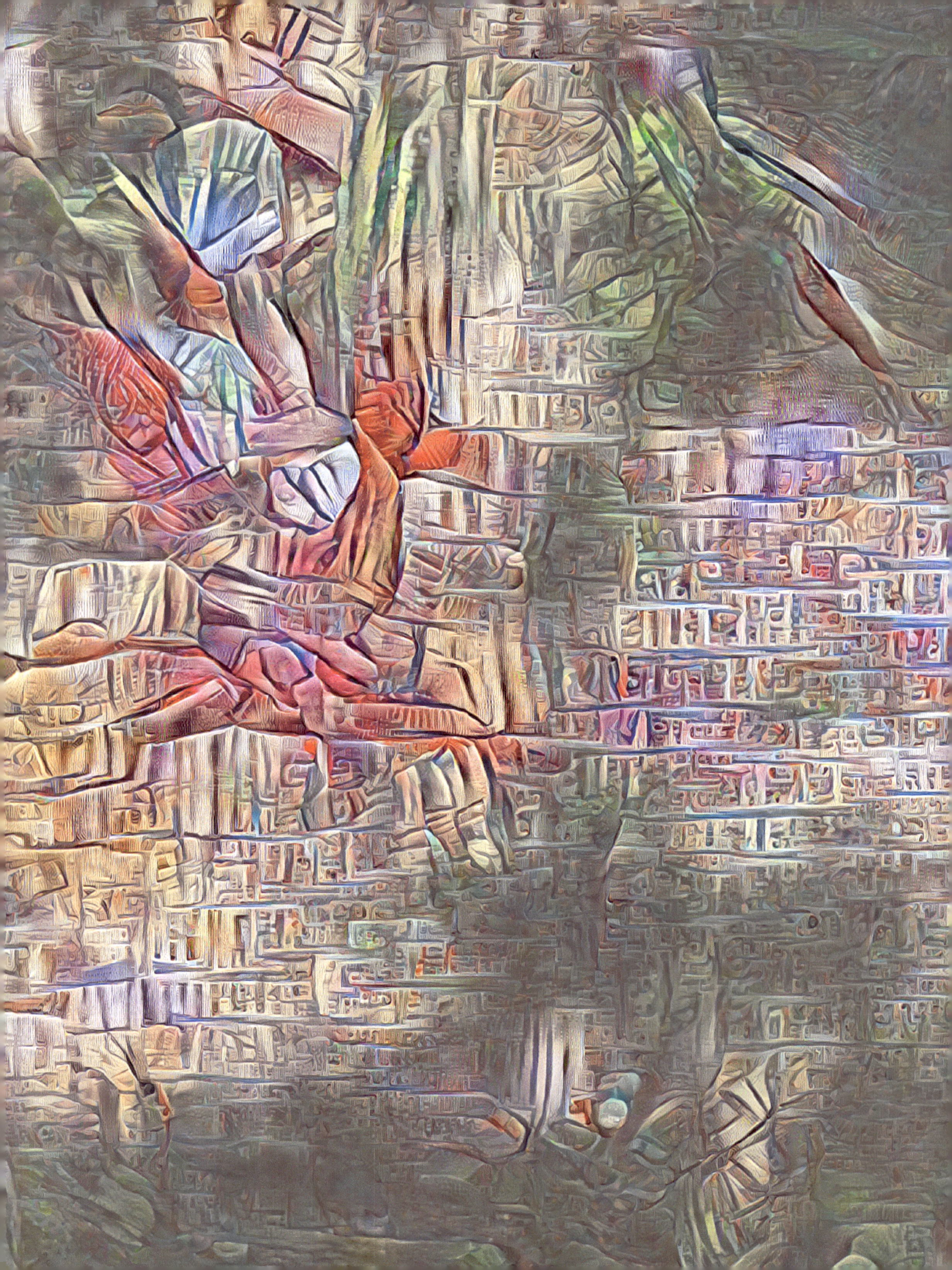

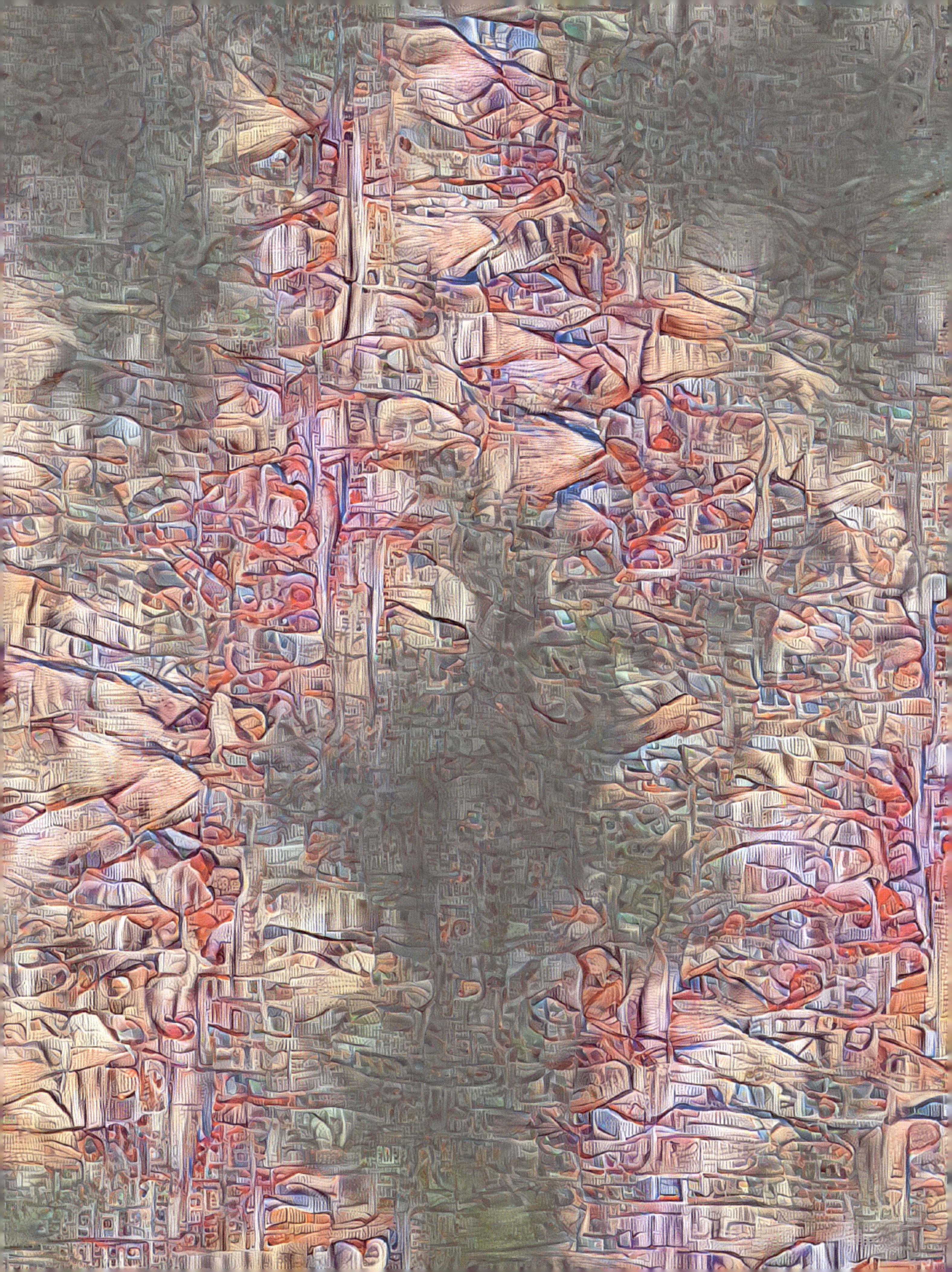

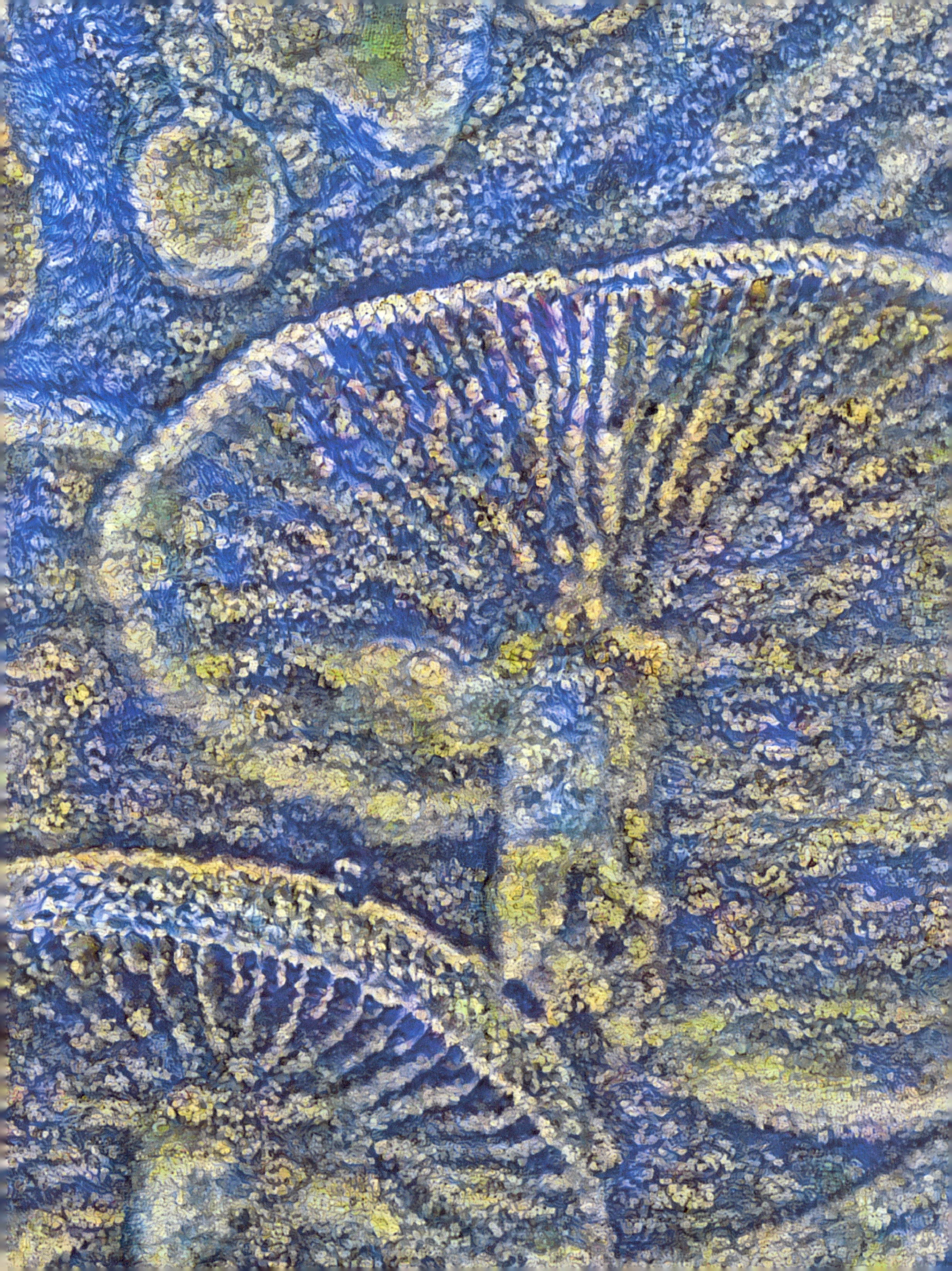

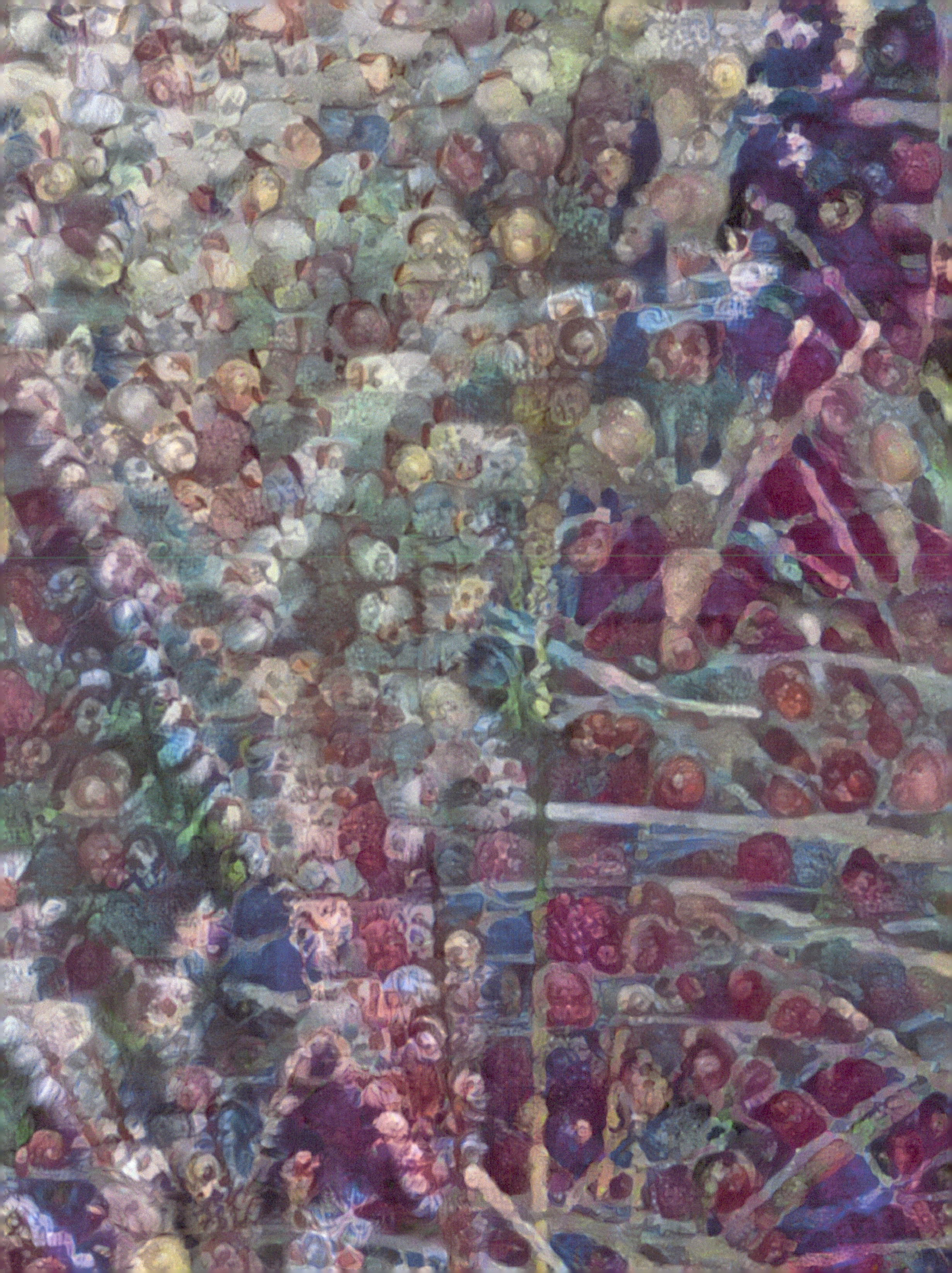

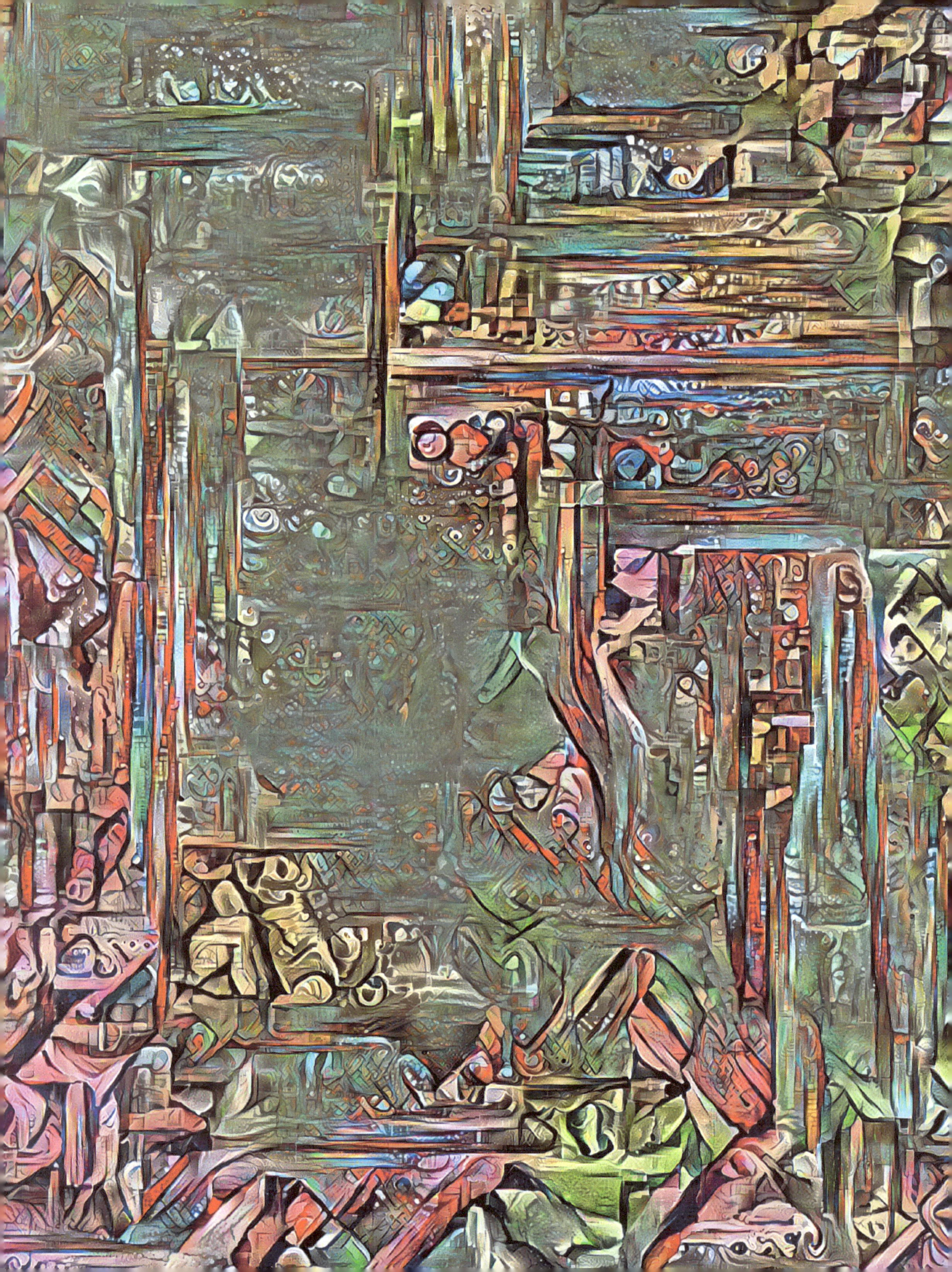

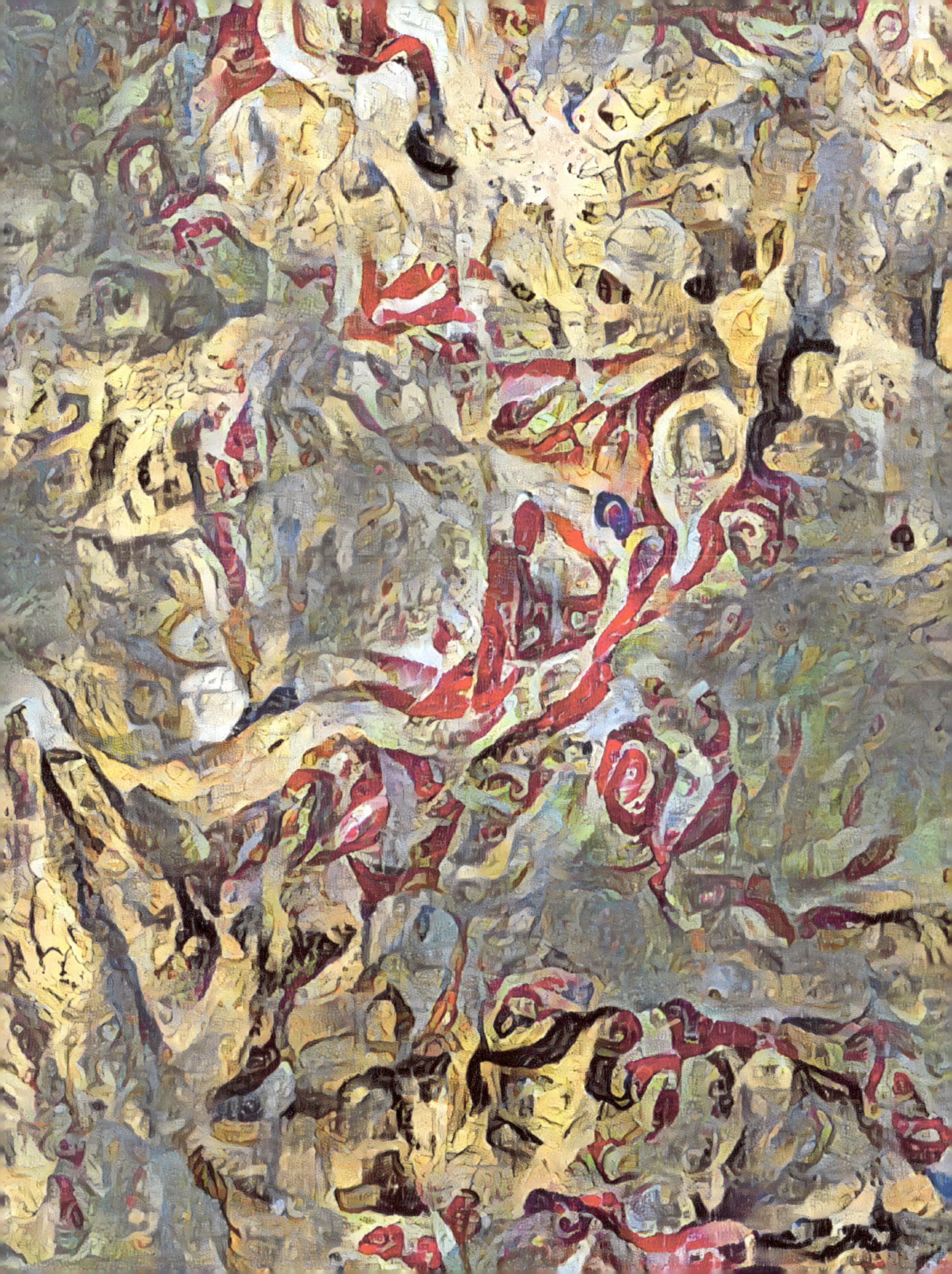

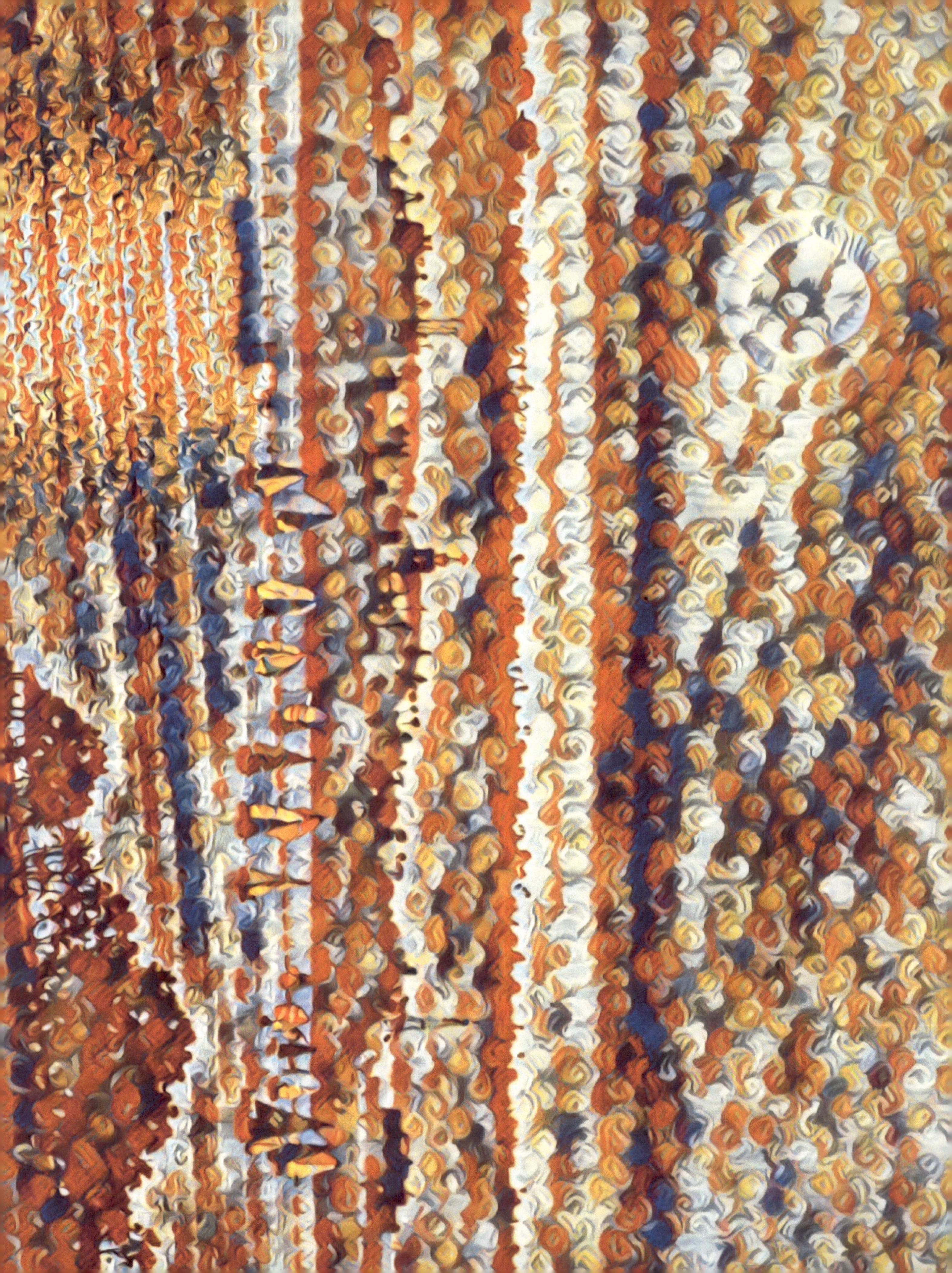

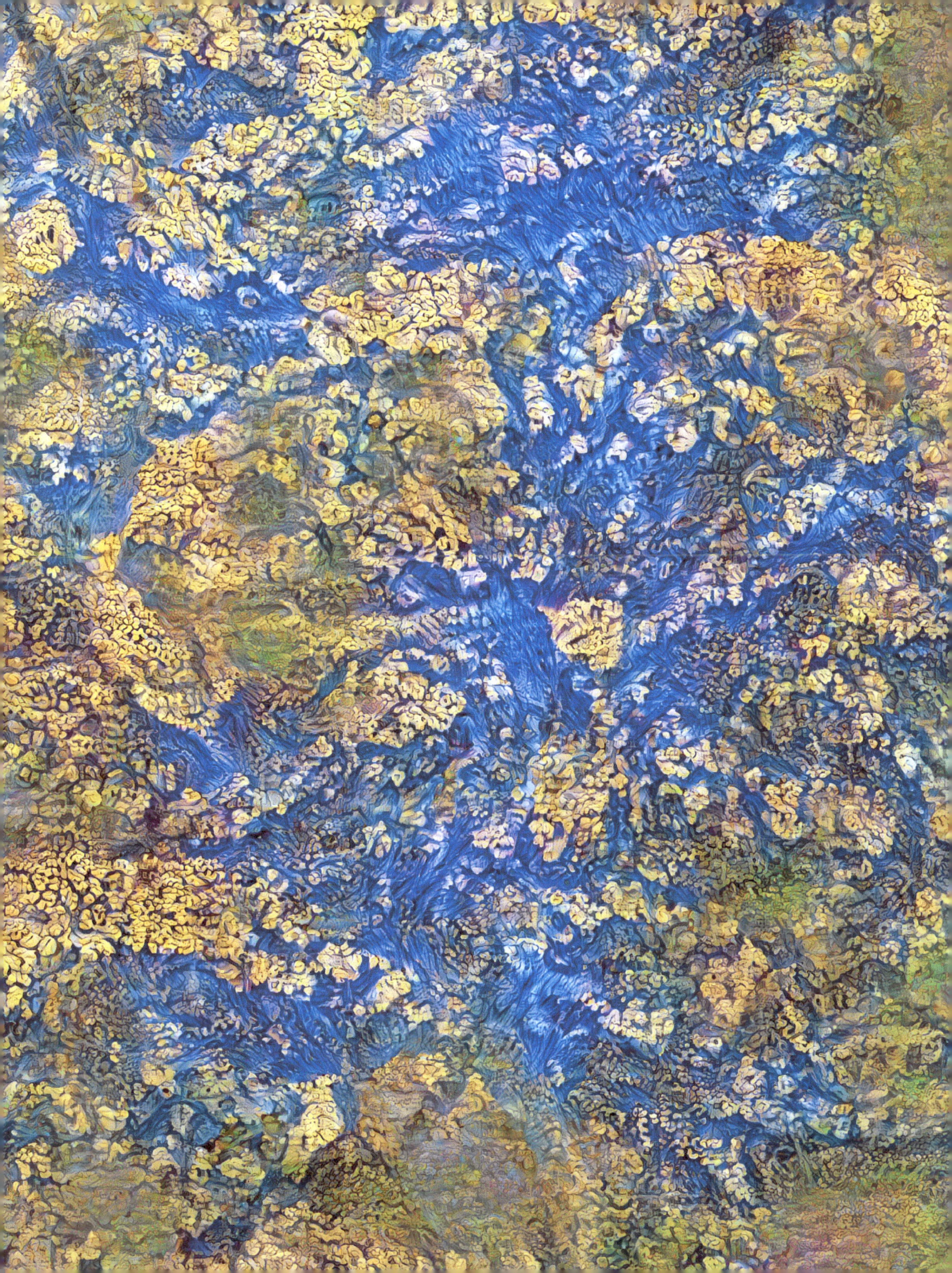

www.ingramcontent.com/pod-product-compliance
Lightning Source LLC
LaVergne TN
LVHW070137110826
845147LV00002B/272
9781735097756